David Whitwell

On the Performance
of the Music
# of Mozart

WITH STYLISTIC PRINCIPLES OF PERFORMANCE

Maxime's Music

Contents

4

List of Figures

6

Preface

IN 1972 I ATTENDED A CONDUCTING WORKSHOP in Phoenix,
Arizona, taught by the then conductor of the Dallas Symphony,
Eduardo Mata (1942–1995). In the course of very fine teaching
he mentioned the importance of thorough study of the master
composers and here he discussed, as an example, how to
perform a specific cadence in the music of Mozart.

I was startled by this discussion, of a performance practice
which sounded so right and authentic, by the fact that I had
never before heard of this practice. After the class I asked him
privately where he learned of this practice and he replied as
a student of the Conservatory in Mexico City. This further
startled me; how could he have learned something in Mexico
City which I had never learned at the University of Michigan or
the Akademie für Music in Vienna?

From this experience I learned that not all important information is found in books and I began to realize that there are
"strings of knowledge" which begin, let us say, in Vienna and
are passed down teacher to student, person to person until
they reach you. If this string is broken, as it had been on this
topic with me, then you may never know some vital piece of
information. Now I also recalled my mother telling me that
she had studied with a pupil of Liszt who at the end of his life
gave a number of his students private information on how to
perform his music, a separate composition for each student

to carry forward. In my mother's case this information was passed down from her teacher to her and then to her own students regarding Liszt's *Liebestraum* which she memorized and played in public for seventy years.

I mention this to make a very important point. If at some time you hear an idea from a teacher or a friend or from this book which you have never before heard, it is very important that you pay attention, give consideration to and retain this information for it may be one of these ancient strings of knowledge passed down and not found in books and you would not want to be responsible for this string ending with you!

Finally, taking advantage of this being the author's preface, I want to add a few personal words about Mozart. Over the course of several decades I have had four occasions when I experienced an extrasensory association with Mozart and I would like to close by sharing two of these. I relate these experiences without explanation and I leave it to the reader to think what he may.

In 1968 my wife and I moved to Vienna, where I joined the Akademie für Music conducting class and explored guest conducting opportunities with European radio orchestras. We decided that if we were going to live in Vienna, we wanted to live *in* Vienna and not out in the suburbs. Fortunately we were able to find a small apartment in the center, walking distance from the famous cathedral. From the first minute I entered this apartment I felt the presence of Mozart and I thought, "Well it is because of my first visit to Vienna and all over town there are plaques reading 'Beethoven lived here,' or 'Mozart lived here,' etc." But for an entire year this presence never left me! Twenty years later, back in Los Angeles, I acquired a new book entitled, *1791: Mozart's Last Year.*[1] In this book was a reproduction of a map of the center of Vienna in 1791. In these old European cities the basic building blocks remain for years, while the street names change, and so it was only in looking at this old map that I discovered that my old apartment was in the same

[1] H. C. Robbins Landon, *1791: Mozart's Last Year.*

building block, and on the same floor, as the apartment in which Mozart had died.

The other occasion was in 1991 when all of Europe was honoring the 200th anniversary of the death of Mozart with concerts. In Los Angeles, of course, there was no notice taken of this anniversary and so I decided, I at least, would honor this moment by creating an evening gathering for my students. Mozart died five minutes after midnight on 4 December 1791, and so for the evening of December 4–5, I planned an event whereby we would all watch again together the recent movie, *Amadeus,* following which I would read from some material I had gathered over the years which quoted first-hand memories by people who actually knew Mozart describing his personality, his free-time activities, how he walked, what he looked like when he ate, etc., in an attempt to make this famous man seem more like a real person for my students. Following this at exactly five minutes after midnight we would have a moment of silence on the 200th anniversary of Mozart's death. This would conclude the event, but anticipating this would be a popular party and that the students would want to stay and visit, I bought hundreds of donuts and with a great department coffee urn made about fifty cups of coffee.

Events went as planned and it was all very moving, however, in planning this evening I had neglected to remember that this evening came during the semester final exam week for the students and consequently only a small number of students could attend. Thus, after all my work planning this event in Mozart's memory, I was feeling very sorry for myself for going to all the trouble and expense and at about 1:00 AM in the morning I was left alone to clean up the large rehearsal room before its use the following day.

After cleaning the room, I had to dispose of all the donuts and all the coffee in the large coffee urn. The coffee urn I had to carry to another building to a faculty room where I could pour out the coffee and wash the large urn. So, picture me duck-walking carrying this heavy urn full of coffee between my legs, as I crossed a patio to the outside doors which led to the faculty room. This was long before the invention that we experience today when we approach a company's doors and they automatically open. These were very heavy steel doors with a bar one had to push to disengage the locking mechanism. As I approached the doors from about five feet away I was thinking, "I guess I am going to have to set the urn down, open the door with one hand while sliding the urn through to get in." At that moment, with no one in sight, both doors opened and after I walked through they closed. Also at this moment, inside the hall, I felt a small, cool breeze which arrived with the thought that Mozart had opened the doors, to thank me for going to all the trouble.

This last characteristic particularly startled me because I recalled a passage in I Kings 19:12 where, in all English translations, one reads that God spoke to Eliljah in a "still small voice." But this is a gloss. In the earliest written version, the 5th century Latin based on earlier manuscripts, known as the Vulgate, God's voice is described as a light breeze [*Sibilus aurae tenuis*].

David Whitwell
2022

Foreword

CRAIG DABELSTEIN is one of the most active music teachers and performers in Australia. In addition to his extensive musical and educational background he became interested in the field of music publication and received a Graduate Certificate of Editing and Publishing from the University of Southern Queensland. This interest, together with his desire to see the publication of better music for wind bands, led him to found a new band publication company for this purpose. During the course of the past few years his company has been praised by band conductors throughout the world and has made his name widely known internationally.

Because of his broad skills I was pleased to agree in 2010 to permit him to publish new editions of my own books. The quality of his work in this regard had been widely praised. I profoundly appreciate his work on my books and music and am particularly impressed in this, his current publication, my book on the performance of the music of Mozart.

David Whitwell
2022

THE PERIOD FROM THE DEATH OF MOZART in 1791 up to the First World War of 1914 can be characterized as a pinnacle in the performance of music. Not only did we see the establishment of the world's great repertoire orchestras but also countless civic and military wind bands, brass bands and choirs populated cities throughout the world. Even a cursory look at a European library catalog, such as that in the Bibliothèque Nationale de France or the Berlin Staatsbibliothek, will reveal literally thousands of compositions from this period.

However, despite this amazing amount of music making in the eighteenth and nineteenth centuries, we have only limited information on how these compositions should be performed, or how they should be edited for modern ensembles. Ironically, we possibly know more about the performance practices of earlier periods, such as the Baroque, than we do about the performance practices of the nineteenth century. Issues such as the peformance of ornaments, the role of the musician to "finish" a composition by applying standard articulations, the instrumentation (what size ensemble did the composer have in mind), are among the topics that need to be considered when performing music from the eighteenth and nineteenth centuries.

This book aims to fill some of that knowledge gap, to enable conductors and performers to recognise and understand the issues in recreating music from this period: not just works by the great masters but also much of the religious, functional and civic music that lives in the libraries of Europe.

Dr David Whitwell's studies of Mozart began with his Ph.D. dissertation (1963) on the early symphonies of Mozart, which included an extensive study of pre-Classical composers and the early development of the sonata form.

He was employed by Universal Edition in Vienna in 1968 to help with the Urtext edition of the first seven Mozart sonatas. He held private discussions at this time with Christa Landon, a Schubert authority; Alexander Weinmann in Vienna, the authority on early Viennese music prints; Ludwig Finscher, the authority on the Classical string quartet; and Françoise Lesure, Director of the Music Division of the National Library of Paris.

While living in Vienna in 1968 Dr. Whitwell was credited as the discoverer of the vast body of eighteenth-century Harmoniemusik repertoire for eight winds. This was followed during his residence for two years in Salzburg with clinics and discussions with members of several professional octets, including those from the Stuttgart Radio Orchestra, the Vienna Symphony, the Brabant Orchestra, as well as the National Orchestra of Peru in Lima, and the Los Angeles Philharmonic.

Dr. Whitwell has given workshops on Mozart performance practice for the students at the Royal College of Music in London and the Conservatory of Music in Milano. He has given a public address on Mozart's κ. 375 at the University of Wisconsin and public lectures in Boston and in Buenos Aires, Argentina. He was the master teacher for a Chamber Music Festival in Santa Fe dedicated to the performance of Mozart's κ. 375, κ. 388 and κ. 361.

David Whitwell has authored articles on Mozart manuscripts in leading journals, including *Music & Letters,* the *Mozart Jahrbuch* and the *London Musical Times,* which was honored by its inclusion in the Garland Library of the History of Western Music, a 1985 collection of the most outstanding articles of musicology.

Whitwell's work on Mozart's Serenade No. 10 for winds in B-flat Major, "Gran Partita," κ. 361, is acknowledged in the preface of the Library of Congress' publication of the facsimile of the autograph score (1976). He is also credited, with regard to the "Gran Partita," κ. 361, with having discovered the proof that this partita has always been one single work and not two separate works as suspected by many earlier scholars, and for discovering the measure to be omitted before the coda of the "Romance" movement.

Whitwell has discussed Mozart performance practice in conducting clinics in Korea, Taiwan, Portugal, Germany, Austria, Switzerland, Hungary, Belgium and Spain.

This book outlines some of the multiple issues of performance practice in the Classical Period and presents them in such a way as to be widely understood by modern conductors and performers. It is relevant, not just to performers of Mozart's music, but also for Mozart's contemporaries and those composers who followed him in the next century.

Craig Dabelstein
2022

Part I

PERFORMANCE PRACTICE IN THE MUSIC OF MOZART

Did Mozart notate staccato?

In 1968 when I was living in Vienna, studying in the conductor's program at the Academy für Music, the famous publisher, Universal Edition, was preparing to create an Urtext version of the Mozart piano sonatas and I was hired to create the first working draft of the first seven sonatas. Over the years I have had the opportunity to examine more than two hundred unfinished autograph manuscripts by Mozart, enough to have some recognition of how he placed notes on paper. Clearly he began with melody and in the unfinished works the melody tends to spin out a number of measures over the rest of a blank score. Next he wrote the bass line, to organize the harmony. These two functions seem to have been his highest interest and most of the rest often appears hastily done, sometimes almost as if he was bored. Here in filling in inner voices one finds stems on note heads going the wrong direction and occasional errors in transposition of horn parts.

This background of my experience caused me to notice in one of the sonatas a passage consisting of two bars of descending diatonic eighth-notes, which appeared to me to be intended to have staccato dots over each note. After the notes had been put on paper, then Mozart began adding the dots, which began clearly formed but as the passage continued the dots came to reflect haste and ended up with several having scratch marks going down below the dot as if he was in too much hurry to lift the pen off the paper. Therefore, in my draft for Universal

Edition, I corrected these to become all clearly formed dots. The chief editor disagreed, believing Mozart intended the final two marks to be vertical stroke signs, a form of strong accent. To settle this dispute, he sent me to visit with Christa Landon, a young woman who was rapidly becoming recognized as the authority of the music of Schubert and whom the editor considered to be an authority in notation of the period. Upon knocking on her door, she appeared holding a small dog which was screaming while Christa was distraught. I immediately discovered a thorn in the dog's paw and removed it, thus becoming a friend for life of Christa.[2]

Ms Landon, after astonishing me by producing manuscripts of eighteen unknown waltzes for Harmoniemusik by Schubert which she had found and was preparing to publish, solved the problem I brought to her. She was the first person who had ever told me that the dot over a note in Mozart meant an accent, the smallest accent Mozart knew how to write, and not staccato. It is one of the problems in Mozart study that he did not clearly distinguish between kinds of accents. We know the basic symbol for an accent for Mozart was the *fp*, but the volume of this accent changed according to the volume of the music at the moment. Beyond the *fp*, Mozart used *sfp* and sometimes both in the same measure where instruments have the identical music.[3] If Mozart had in mind some distinction between *fp* and *sfp*, we do not know what it was.

A clear example I think can be seen in the final cadence of the Romance movement of the "Gran Partita," K. 361. Here, where the basic rhythmic vehicle is the quarter-note, Mozart has written eighth-notes with eighth-rests, that is, a written out form of the modern staccato, yet each note also has a dot above it to add an accent (Figure 2). The dot could not mean the modern staccato because Mozart had already notated that.

Historically, we can say that there is evidence that at the time Mozart lived the concept of a dot over a note meaning an accent seems to have been established. In K. P. E. Bach's *Essay*

[2] Unfortunately, soon afterwards she died in the crash, on land, of two 747s, killing 550 people.

[3] See Figure 1, mm. 17 and 18 in the third variation of the Theme and Variations of the "Gran Partita," K. 361.

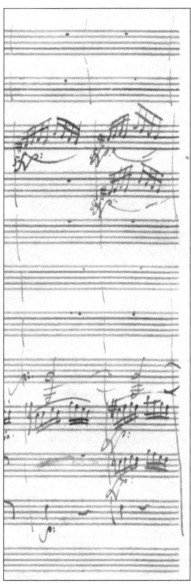

Figure 1: Mozart, "Gran Partita," Theme and Variations, mm. 17–18.

on the True Art of Playing Keyboard Instruments, first published about the time of Mozart's birth, Bach reports,

> Attack and touch are one and the same thing. Everything depends on their force and duration. When notes are to be detached from each other, strokes or dots are placed above them.

Curiously enough, when Bach refers to regular unmarked notes he seems to describe how we today define the word "staccato."

> Tones which are neither detached, connected, nor fully held are sounded for half their value.

Before this time there can be found many musical examples of the use of the dot to mean an accent in the repertoire of the seventeenth-century German Hautboisten bands. In Figure 3, the Ouverture,[4] fourth movement, Aria, one can see how accented eighth-notes would help propel the motion forward, whereas staccato eighth-notes would be like marking time.

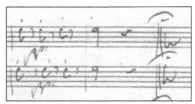

Figure 2: Mozart, "Gran Partita," Romance, mm. 129–130.

[4] D-HRD Fü 3741a, Nr. 25

Figure 3: Ouverture [D-HRD Fü 3741a, Nr. 25], IV. Aria, mm. 1–8.

Another example from the Hautboisten repertoire is quite interesting. This example (Figure 4), found in the first movement of a *Concerto da camera*[5] which is thought to have been composed

[5] D-HRD Fü 3741a, Nr. 8

by Kapellmeister Sydow, who was appointed head of a military school founded by Frederick the Great, demonstrates the use of the dot to increase the volume of the lower notes of the octave leaps and demonstrates the knowledge at the time of what we call today the "pyramid principle." Since the Renaissance, music treatises have commented on the fact that lower notes need to be performed stronger in order to balance the upper voices. This application is very clear in this example.

Figure 4: Concerto da Camera [D-HRD Fü 3741a, Nr. 8], I. Allegro, mm. 7–10.

Another very interesting early example of the use of a dot to represent an accent is found in one of the greatest of all early original band compositions, the *Requiem for Louis XVI and Marie Antoinette* of 1815 for large band and chorus by Charles Bochsa.[6] At the end of the Recordare movement we see quarter-notes with dots, but also under a slur which at first glance would seem to contradict the purpose of the dot. The *Elson's Music Dictionary* of 1905[7] gives an identical illustration under the discussion of "Portamento." The usual understanding of portamento is a very connected style, but here Elson notes that for singers, who need to have at the same time clear syllables, we should change the name of this term to "demi-marcato." Elson calls this a "pressing accent" referring to the voice. In the

[6] Bochsa was a harpist and court composer in Paris.

[7] p. 208

Bochsa example which follows, although there are no syllables, perhaps a "pressing" effect such as Elson describes might be adopted.

Figure 5: Bochsa, *Requiem*, Recordare, mm. 81–88.

A final example of the use of the dot to mean adding an accent, rather than treating it as a modern staccato, we quote to indicate that by the middle of the nineteenth century this concept was still understood. This illustration is found in one of the great original band works, the *Begrabnisgesang*, op. 13, of 1858 for band and chorus by Brahms. Here we have the entire band and chorus performing at full volume, marked *ff*. In order to make the faster articulations underneath in the low brass and timpani cut through all this sound, Brahms gives them the staccato dots.

Figure 6: Brahms, *Begrabnisgesang,* op. 13, mm. 33–35.

Finally, at the end of the nineteenth century one finds this practice still known. In what was for many years the standard reference book on music, *Elson's Music Dictionary* (1905), p. 5, we read,

> The staccato mark is sometimes used merely as an accent mark (percussive) as may be seen in the closing theme of Beethoven's "Sonate Pathetique" first movement, and in much other modern music.

Figure 7: Beethoven, *Sonate Pathetique,* op. 13, Grave–Allegro di molto e con brio, mm. 303–307

Regarding this long use of the dot to mean an accent, I think something very natural is happening here. Try singing a string of quarter-notes with the syllable "lu" at a tempo of quarter-note = 60. You will notice the ear concentrates on the last half of each quarter, for that and its connection with the following note is what makes it legato. Now, reduce each quarter by half, still at quarter-note = 60, and you will notice that now the ear has its focus on the beginning of the note, not on the end, and you will hear the impression of an accent on the beginning of each note. And you will find that there is nothing you can do not to sing this accent. So this impression of a short note appearing to have an accent may have been the origin of the dot over the note meaning an accent in earlier music.

The question might arise that since the dot creates the same physical effect, perhaps it is only just a distinction in language that we call one staccato and the other an accent. The answer is "No," because music is more than either what is on paper or a physical sound. Music is also a form of emotional and psychological communication which cannot be notated on paper. To illustrate this, let us return to the Mozart κ. 361 Romance movement mentioned above.

In the final cadence of the Romance movement we see in the next to last measure three eighth-notes, each with a dot above, in the context of a written *ritard*.[8] (See Fig. 8). Thus we see,

[8] In another place we will explain Mozart's notation of *ritard*.

Figure 8: Mozart, "Gran Partita," Romance, mm. 129–130.

> note note note final note.

A true staccato has an uplift feeling as part of its quality, which might be expressed on a string instrument by up bow symbols or in the tip of a baton showing an uplift bounce on each beat, thus,

> up up up final note.

On the other hand, a true accent has a heavier downward gravitational quality, which might be expressed on a string instrument with down bow symbols or in the tip of the baton making small *tenuto* movements, a downward gesture in the tip of the baton caused by the wrist. Here the effect would be like three steps going down stairs.

> down down down final note.

Two quite different psychological and emotional results, between which the musician must make a choice. But how do we know which is correct, or which Mozart had in mind? The answer cannot be found on paper, for notation is incapable of making this distinction. That is why, in German, what the conductor and players look at is called *Die Noten*, not *Die Musik*.

One must get away from the score, perhaps sitting on a sofa and hearing the music in one's mind and maybe singing it to one's self. If one does this, one of the most fundamental basic qualities of music, Universality, will come into play. It is most likely that the version which seems "right" to you, on the basis of feeling, will also be the one which feels right to the players and most likely is the way Mozart also felt. You can bet your last dollar on this because scientists of comparative physiology and anatomy believe that while everything in the external world has changed in the past three hundred years, the basic emotions have not.

What did Mozart mean by "Adagio?"

It might be a good time to employ the new practice of using
Italian words, such as adagio, presto, etc.
    —Michael Praetorius[9]

[9] *Syntagma musicum*, 1619, III, 51.

An Adagio indicates distress.
    —Johann Mattheson[10]

[10] *Der vollkommene Capellmeister*, 1739, II, xii, 34ff.

It is true that at the beginning of every piece special words are
written which are designed to characterize it, such as "Allegro"
(merry), "Adagio" (slow) and so on. But both slow and quick
have their degrees ... So one has to deduce the tempo from the
piece itself, and it is this by which the true worth of a musician
can be recognized without fail.
    —Leopold Mozart[11]

[11] *Violinschule*, 1756, I, iii, 7.

HAVING SEEN, IN FEWER THAN TWENTY YEARS, the definition
of *Adagio* go from "distress" to "slow," the father of Mozart
seemed to indicate that perhaps it is better to ignore the Italian
words at the beginning of a composition and to determine the
tempo by studying the music itself. Let the music tell you the
tempo, he says. I would rephrase that for today's student to
read, "Think not how the music speaks to your calculator, but
rather how the music speaks to your heart."

But Leopold Mozart's advice is not an easy lesson for some
musicians to learn because the very fact of the eye looking at
printed data tends to circumvent the world of emotion from
which the music evolved.

Figure 9: Mozart, "Gran Partita," K. 361, Theme and Variations

I am thinking, for example, of a passage in the great "Gran Partita," K. 361 of Mozart, the fifth variation in the Theme and Variations movement (see Fig. 8). Here the conductor sees in the introduction written for Basset horns a repetitive figure, little more than a tremulo, written in 32nd-notes. Since the tempo is given as *Adagio,* and considering the fact that 32nd-notes were rarely seen by the wind players of this time, some conductors seem inclined to give a very slow tempo. This results in two problems. First, in a very slow tempo these 32nd-notes now call attention to themselves as melodic material, which they are not. Most important, and certainly most important to Mozart, at a very slow tempo the lovely lyric oboe solo above this harmonic texture is pulled apart and fails to take flight. My advice here is for the conductor, in his study, to sing this oboe melody at varying speeds until he finds a tempo in which the melody seems natural and expressive. Then that must be the tempo of this variation and those accompanying instruments just have to deal with it.

Another example which has bothered me a great deal over the years is performances of the Adagio of the Mozart Clarinet Concerto, which I have heard numerous times (see Fig. 9). A tempo which seems natural, musical and correct to me is one at about quarter-note = 60–65. But I have nearly always heard this performed much slower, often at quarter-note = 50, or even 45, a tempo at which the music is pulled apart and in which the accompanying figures make no sense. The lyrical descending eighth-notes in the viola and second violin in m. 8 begin to sound like mountain goats leaping from one ledge to another.

Figure 10: Mozart, Clarinet Concerto, K. 622, Adagio, mm. 1–9.

Whenever I have (politely) asked the performer how he determined his very slow tempo, the answer has always been the same all over the world, "This is the tempo my teacher plays this movement!" What bothers me more than this answer itself is the fact that I believe we have fallen into a tradition in this country of teaching students to play without at the same time listening to the music itself. In this case the clarinet soloist is completely focused on playing his part and I believe often is not even aware of the strange effects that such a slow tempo has on the rest of the music itself. In my own days as a horn student, playing all those beautiful movements in the Mozart horn concerti, I cannot recall a single occasion when the teacher asked what I was feeling, or what I thought about the music. Not to mention etudes! I am reminded of a famous story about a horn player, Bruno Jaenicke, who was principal horn in the

New York Philharmonic at the turn of the twentieth century.
An admirer at the time asked him what he was thinking about
when he was producing such beautiful music. Did he imagine
beautiful landscape scenes, or think of beautiful women? He
answered, I think, "get this note—get this note" etc.

Another composition that has made me want to learn more
about what Mozart was thinking in using the word "Adagio" is
one of his last works, the beautiful "Ave verum Corpus," K. 618,
for chorus and orchestra. It is written in alla breve, meaning to
be conducted in two, but the vehicle which carries the music
is the quarter-note. Most performances I have heard are at the
tempo of quarter-note = 70–74, which seems rather fast to be
an Adagio.

In 2017 I was giving a clinic to clarinet students at the Conser-
vatorio in Milano, Italy, on the performance practice of Mozart,
and afterwards, having coffee with my host, I mentioned that if
I were able to meet Mozart is some after-life the one question
I would ask him, relative to this tempo concern, is, "What did
you mean by Adagio?"

My host immediately answered, "But he was using a completely different word!" He was using the word "agio," which
means "at your leisure" or "as you wish," or as the conductor
and musicians felt the music. That certainly makes sense. I
then asked several ordinary persons on the street of Milan
and found this word was still in common usage and with the
same meaning, "as you like it". And, one must recall that as a
teenager Mozart had three separate long residences in Milan,
totaling more than a year's time. It seems clear to me that
Milan was where he learned his Italian.

The formation is as follows: the first "a" is a preposition. Then,
since "agio" would entail adjacent vowels, a's, an elision
("suppression of a vowel or syllable") was made by inserting a
"d" to separate them, in the same way as in French, l'amour is
substituted for la amour, for the same reason. Thus: a–d–agio.

Several correspondents in Italy have written to say the modern usage of "agio" is to convey a state of comfort or to relax. This is an example of what philologists talk about in languages being living things which change. My very professional *Cassell Italian–English Dictionary,* revised in 1967, does not use these words at all and of course does not use the "distress" found in 1739. The point of my quest, of course, is not modern Italian, but in wondering what it meant in Mozart's eighteenth-century Italian. But I am happy to accept my correspondents "comfort" in saying I now have more comfort in understanding Mozart's intent.

Why do we never see the word ritard. in the scores of Mozart?

In 2006 I was engaged as the master teacher for an adult chamber music festival in Santa Fe, New Mexico. The wind players were all professional level artists and they engaged me to discuss the Mozart wind partitas, even though they had performed these compositions many times during their careers.

I elected to begin the first rehearsal with the Andante movement of the Partita in C Minor, K. 388. After a very intense and contemplative development section, the recapitulation ends with two eighth-notes, marked *pp*, whereas the end of the Exposition section these two eighth-notes are not only marked *f*, but also with a stroke accent, the strongest kind of accent Mozart used. I used to wonder if perhaps Mozart wanted to end this introspective movement with two suddenly soft eighth-notes as if to put his finger to his lips to whisper "don't tell," or some other personal closing comment for the listener. But this never sounded or felt "right," especially as the two eighth-notes, written without articulation marks tend to run together, giving a rather confused effect. So on this first reading in Santa Fe, with players who knew the music and were skilled enough to do anything I conducted, I decided to conduct this ending the way I had always felt it should end, making those last two eighth-notes spaced out, as if part of a real *rallentando*. The effect for the listeners, the players and I, was like leaning back and emitting a sigh, allowing the listener to release the tension which builds up in this very personal movement. These mature professional players who had performed this work for decades all suddenly cried out, "How did you know to do that? That has to be right!"

What happened here? A group of very experienced musicians all performed something not indicated on paper and yet it seemed "right." The answer I think is again found in the Italian language. My professional *Cassell Dictonary* not only says that *pp* can mean either very soft or very slow, a single *p* can be soft, or gentle or slow. Today we have almost entirely lost the tradition that a *p* can mean slow, although there is one instance in which we all use that meaning. In the great body of late Baroque and early Classical Period forms the fast–slow–fast three-movement format is the most common and the second movements nearly always begin with a marking of *p*, which we take for granted to mean "slow." Not a single one of us has ever told a class, "We will now hear the 'soft' movement of the Mozart Symphony Nr. 40."

It is interesting that in agreeing with me that Mozart's use of *p* or *pp* in a cadence might mean slower, not softer, the great Schubert scholar, Dr. Walter Dürr, of the *Neue Schubert-Ausgabe*, wrote me that Schubert used *decrescendo* to mean get softer, but that he used *diminuendo* to mean softer and slower about 90% of the time.

One wonders then why did Mozart not simply write *ritardando*, or *ritard.*? As it turns out he never did! In all the extant autograph scores in Mozart's hand, more than six hundred of them, there is not one single place where he wrote *ritard*! But this, in turn, raises another question. Mozart, who wrote such sensitive music, music appreciated by nearly all who knew it, had the experience of having his music performed by the greatest musicians in Europe at that time, including those of Vienna, London, Prague and Paris. It seems beyond belief that the finest musicians in Europe, performing six hundred compositions, never in a single instance ever performed a *ritard*.

anywhere in any performance of any of these scores! These questions are resolved if they knew, as I have now concluded, that a **p** or **pp** appearing in a Mozart cadence meant *ritard.*

A very strong argument for my contention is found in the ending of the first movement of the Piano Concerto in A Major, K. 488. Here the reader will see following a typical *forte*, noisy ritornello to close the movement, suddenly one final measure marked *piano*. It's like running into a wall and looks so strange, standing by itself, that if we did not have the autograph score we might think it a printer's error to see a single measure of *piano* at the end of the movement. But since there is no important melodic material in this bar and only cadential figuration, we must believe Mozart simply wanted the music to just slow down as it drifts off. One European conductor/friend says it reminds him of one of those older cars where you turn the key to off, but the motor continues to run down a bit.

In a previous chapter I have mentioned the final cadence of the Adagio of the "Gran Partita," K. 361. By making the final of the three repeated cadential fragments a very drawn out real *rallentando*, it becomes a perfectly beautiful cadence, one with the elegance one has come to expect in Mozart, and which, as in the case above of the final cadence of the Andante of the Partita, K. 388, results in a kind of musical sigh, allowing the listener to release the long tension built up by this movement. In fact, it is my opinion that the slower one plays the final measure of this Adagio the more elegant and musical it sounds.

In the autograph score for the Romance movement of the "Gran Partita," K. 361, we see a cadence where Mozart was quite precise.

In the bottom staves, mm. 22–23, we see *piano crescendo forte*. The *piano* in the following measure is not part of a **fp** accent, but rather is used to show that the cadence from this point on is a *ritard.* (see Fig. 10). Here the *ritard.* is very important for it makes a smooth transition to a slower tempo for the Allegretto and a more musical result for the soli bassoons. In

Figure 11: Mozart, "Gran Paritia," K. 361, Romance, mm. 22–24.

most performances today, which do not make a *ritard.*, the following Allegretto at a faster tempo, renders the soli bassoons sounding like some kind of out of control noisy machine.

Finally, I hasten to point out that Mozart in the normal course of his composition did still use the *p* and *pp* in the sense we understand today, to mean soft or softer. But having said that I believe one must always be careful in Mozart and stop to ask "does this *p* mean soft or slower?" I am thinking of places in the first movements of Mozart's horn concerti where in the middle of a movement there is a section which I always had felt should be played a bit slower, but I was never allowed to do so by my teachers. But one must remember that this practice also had a long tradition. Carl Maria von Weber, whose musical education coincided in time with Mozart's period of composition, stated,

There is no slow tempo in which passages do not occur that demand a quicker motion, so as to obviate the impression of dragging. Conversely there is no presto that does not need

a quiet delivery in many places, so as not to throw away the
chance of expressiveness by hurrying.

Improvisation in the Music of Mozart

IN THINKING ABOUT THIS SUBJECT there are first some important historical things one must keep in mind. First, before the period of notation in the late Middle Ages, there were distant centuries when all music was improvisation and the performer was also the composer.

The role of the performer remained more important than some people today realize when the performance of music was practiced in the later period of established court and civic ensembles. During the eighteenth century especially there was a tremendous demand by the aristocrats to have new music, not the performance of older music. Perhaps a fairly common example was Frederick the Great who wanted a new flute concerto to perform every Thursday evening! In this environment the performer remained an active participant in the production of music. The composer with regular players at his disposal knew their strengths and desires as players and could, and in some cases had to, leave details of the composition for the players to finish. This included much of articulation markings, the filling in of leaps and other details of performances including tempo. In the latter case there was the famous occasion during Haydn's first visit to London when, although he was engaged as the composer and the official guest conductor, the first violinist demanded it was his duty to select the tempos.

It was only with the dawn of the nineteenth century that the pendulum of the responsibility for the details of performance swung from the player to the composer. Now it was possible for a violinist to object to Beethoven that his new concerto was too difficult to play, that Beethoven could reply, "Do you think I care about you and your damned fiddle when the spirit is upon me!?" But this new focus on the composer, rather than the player, was already changing in the previous generation, during the lifetime of Mozart. Therefore the modern performer must recall this history of performance and understand that Mozart left some things for the performer to finish. This includes not only details of articulation but also opportunities for the player to improvise and places where the player *must* improvise. The rule for the last category is this: If it sounds like nothing is happening, or that one player did not arrive, then something must be filled in. The most common instance in the Baroque and Classical Periods is when the only thing on paper is an Alberti-bass sequence. Alberti-bass is not music, it is a symbol that improvisation must be added. By the time of Mozart, Alberti-bass is not as common and its place is often taken by repeated triads with no melody. In this regard I must mention the long strings of triads which appear in the piano parts of the Mozart Piano Concerti when the orchestra has the melodic material. This was especially true in the cases where the concerto was written for Mozart to perform himself, in a performance perhaps a week or two later and when during the meantime he might have written several more compositions. I suspect these triads were to remind Mozart of the chords, as he would have been reading from a piano part and not a full score in performance. We cannot know whether in performance Mozart actually played these triads, or whether he just watched them go by as a means of knowing where he was in the composition or if maybe he played something else in their place. My personal belief, given his own great talent in improvisation and in composition, is that he did not play what is on paper. But what should the modern player do?

Figure 12: Mozart, "Gran Paritia," к. 361, Largo, mm. 1 – 5.

In a related practice, and here I am thinking of my own experience with the horn concerti, there are sometimes places
where the soloist has only whole-notes, even several in a row,
and where the orchestra has only accompaniment sounding
music, and not primary melodic or thematic material. I have
felt Mozart expected the soloist to fill in these places where
anything the player did would be more interesting than a
whole-note. This category includes final cadences where the
orchestra is playing repeated chords and the soloist has a long
series of repeated pitches. Even playing triads would be more
musical than playing repeated tones. This falls in the category
mentioned above of the performer finishing the composition.
There are similar passages in the music of this period where
the composer will have a series of sixteenth-notes, then a
whole-note followed by more sixteenth notes. In such a case
I thought that the whole-note offered the wind player a place
to take a breath and then fill in the rest of the measure with
sixteenth-notes.

A similar situation one sees in the manuscripts of this period
is where the composer left it to the player to fill in a gap of a
large leap upward. Here, again, it appears the practice was
well enough established that the player would fill in the leap
with diatonic notes (not improvisation of other material) so
the composer wouldn't have to waste the time and ink to do so.
All those great leaps back and forth at the ends of the Weber
clarinet concerti are a typical example. One very important
example of this practice is found in the Adagio of the Mozart
"Gran Partita," K. 361.

Another case where the player must fill in something is widely
known. This is the case of an eighth-note with an appoggiatura
connected before it, followed by two sixteenth-notes. I think all
players today understand that this is to be played as if it had
been notated as four sixteenth-notes. The reason Mozart wrote
it as he did was to indicate an accent on the first sixteenth-note.

Less known in the US is a general rule that a quarter-note
when followed by rests in the remainder of the measure is

to be performed at one-half its written value. The origin of this practice came from the numerous cases where a melody ended with a quarter-note after the bar line and is played as an eighth-note so that it does not overlap with the entrance of another voice. This is very obvious in the first three measures of the first movement of the "Gran Partita," K. 361, where Mozart would have never expected the beginning of the clarinet solos to be obscured by the ensemble's final quarter-note. This example is particularly interesting since Mozart begins the movement with the ensemble playing the most frequently found instrumental cadence of the Classical Period. The performance practice of the cadence, often called the "Stair-step cadence," was known to all players at the time and should be known by all players today: [1] the first beat is played the strongest, [2] the second beat is double-dotted, and [3] the third beat is played half its value, as an eighth-note (hence no overlap with the clarinet entrance). One has to wonder if this were a subtle example of Mozart's humor, to begin the longest instrumental work he would ever compose with the most famous cadence of the period! By the way, this rule is why Mozart in the very final measure of this movement wrote a half-note—to insure he would get a quarter-note. Modern American conductors who take this final note and turn it into an almost fermata-like grand ending make a great mistake, not only documenting their lack of knowledge of the style but because they leave the listener feeling that there must be still another measure with a final downbeat.

Finally, there are places where Mozart expected, and performance demands, improvisation in his music. A very clear example is found in the first movement of his Quintet for clarinet and strings. Mozart first writes a beautiful and simple melody which is repeated. But connecting this melody and its repetition is a two-measure document of a clarinet player "noodling," meaningless arpeggios up and down which every clarinet player does as soon as he puts his instrument together to try it out. Mozart was writing a solo work for clarinet and all his life he had observed clarinets do this, and so in another example of his sense of humor, Mozart, in composing a solo work for clarinet, introduces the soloist "noodling." It is another characteristic of Mozart that on occasion in development sections he liked to show off his skill, to demonstrate that he could make music out of nothing. Here, in such an example, he composes the entire development section, not out of his beautiful melodies, but out of this "noodling" fragment. Each string player in turn has a written-out improvisation on this fragment, when finally it is the clarinet's turn. Now Mozart says, in effect, it is your turn, you are the soloist now go! And Mozart writes several measures with only one chord tone per beat, making it easy for the soloist to improvise. Surely no clarinet player on earth would fail to improvise here and only actually play these measures of empty chord tones? Yes, they all do! And if you ask them why, they will answer "Oh, but who am I to change something the Master wrote?"

Finally, a more familiar symbol for required improvisation is the use of the fermata sign to indicate the place for a cadenza or an *Eingang*. The appearance of the fermata sign familiar to most musicians is the one usually found in the first movements of concerti of the Classical Period. Typically found just before the final orchestral ritornello, the fermata sign is found over a tonic chord in the second inversion. During the Classical Period it was expected that the soloist would improvise, using the musical materials of the first movement. A valuable list of the eighteenth-century expectations was given by Türk.[12]

[12] D. G. Türk, *Kurze Anweisung zum Generalbassspielen* (Halle, 1791), 166.

1. The cadenza should particularly reinforce the impression the composition has made in a most lively way and present the most important parts of the whole composition in the form of a brief summary or in an extremely concise arrangement.

2. The cadenza, like every extempore embellishment, must consist not so much of intentionally added difficulties as of such thoughts which are most scrupulously suited to the main character of the composition.

3. Cadenzas should not be too long, especially in compositions of a melancholy character.

4. Modulations into other keys, particularly to those which are far removed, either do not take place at all—for example in short cadenzas—or they must be used with much insight and, as it were, only in passing. In no case should one modulate to a key which the composer himself has not used in the composition.

5. Variety is necessary if the attention of the listener is to be held. Therefore as much of the unexpected and the surprising as can possibly be added should be used in the cadenza.

6. No thought should be often repeated in the same key or in another, no matter how beautiful it may be.

7. Every dissonance which has been included, even in single-voiced cadenzas, must be properly resolved.

8. A cadenza does not have to be erudite, but novelty, wit, an abundance of ideas and the like are so much more its indispensable requirements.

9. The same tempo and meter should not be maintained throughout the cadenza ... The whole cadenza should be more like a fantasia which has been fashioned out of an abundance of feeling, rather than a methodically-constructed composition.

10. Even though the cadenza has been carefully written out and memorized, it should be performed as if it were merely invented on the spur of the moment.

The above description reflects the extent to which the concerto had become much more of a public event than it had been in the Baroque Period when such works were performed for select guests in palace rooms. The Baroque cadenza was played as part of the final cadence, on the next to last harmony (dominant) and was much shorter, the rule being what a singer or instrumentalist could do in one breath. The idea was for the artist to have the opportunity to make a final reflection on the feeling of the movement.

The *Eingang,* a name coined by Mozart, was a generally brief improvised passage for the purpose of leading into the next material. And for this reason, it is usually played by the player who has the melody in the following music. Mozart often used this device in places where he seemed concerned that the following music, either in tempo or in style, might be too abrupt for the listener. The *Eingang* is recognized by the appearance of a fermata over a dominant or substitute dominant chord. It is essential that the conductor recognize the distinction in harmony between the cadenza and the *Eingang.* There are many recordings which have been made of Mozart concerti where a cadenza is played where Mozart only intended an *Eingang.* Mozart often wrote out *Eingänge* and one can see an example in the Romance movement of the "Gran Partita," K. 361.

Part II

APPLIED
PERFORMANCE
PRACTICE

Mozart's "Gran Partita," K. 361

THIS IS ONE OF THE GREAT COMPOSITIONS BY MOZART, and is his longest instrumental work. It was composed early in 1784 and before the premiere the word was out, one newspaper writing in advance that the concert would include a "great wind piece of a very special kind composed by Herr Mozart." And indeed a reviewer afterward wrote,

> I heard music for wind instruments today, too, my Herr Mozart, in four movements—glorious and sublime! ... Oh, what an effect it made—glorious and grand, excellent and sublime.

The fact that the work is scored for twelve wind instruments and string bass should pose no surprise for there is a long history of the twelve-member wind band. The *Les Grands Hautboisten* of Louis XIV consisted of twelve players. When this practice spread to Germany, beginning in 1690, those groups were also twelve players, one of whom called themselves, "The Apostles." The Handel *Fireworks* music, which we associate with the huge doublings of the first performance in England, appears in the autograph score as a work for twelve players, eleven winds and timpani. The Gossec *Te Deum,* the earliest work of the French Revolution repertoire was for twelve players on paper. And finally, one can find a number of late eighteenth- and nineteenth-century works composed for a twelve-member ensemble.

First movement, Largo – Molto Allegro

In the very first measure we see one of the important idioms of the Classical style, the "stair-step cadence" with all three of its parts:

1. The first note is played strong. Here, as was the case with many Viennese scores of this period, the beginning is assumed to be *forte*, therefore Mozart did not bother to write *forte* in all voices.

2. The second beat was played as a double-dotted rhythm.

3. The third beat was played half the written value, as if an eighth-note.[13]

[13] For a more elegant effect I slur the third and fourth notes.

Figure 13: Mozart, "Gran Partita," к. 361, m. 1, manuscript.

Figure 14: Mozart, "Gran Partita," к. 361, m. 1, with applied performance practice.

Because the fourth note is in the practice of this cadence now an eighth-note, notice that it is out of the way and does not conflict with the solo clarinet's entrance. It demonstrates that Mozart was aware of the Viennese custom of making a note followed by rests one-half of its written value. Nothing would be gained by blotting out the soloist's entrance. For the solo Mozart has written *dolce,* a term he used as we would write today "solo part."

Notice also in the first measure Mozart needed one more note to complete the diatonic line and so he added it as a grace note in m. 2. Since grace notes were played before the beat, this grace note serves as part of the diatonic scale. There is absolutely nothing in the style of this period which would suggest a Baroque appoggiatura here or any other solution which makes this grace note become part of the first beat of m. 2. It was also out of the style, and likewise it would have never occurred to Mozart to create a quintuplet to accommodate this needed extra note. The soloist simply works the extra note in smoothly or the players just wait—a very common practice in the late Baroque internal cadences.

Figure 15: Mozart, "Gran Partita," K. 361, m. 1, solo entrance, manuscript.

Figure 16: Mozart, "Gran Partita," K. 361, m. 1, solo entrance with applied performance practice.

There is a very minor performance problem in mm. 12 and 13. Arithmetically speaking, the first note of the third and fourth beats of the basset horns is not long enough to allow the listener to hear the harmonic resolution in the oboe part. The conductor needs to have the basset horn players play these notes slightly longer, until their ear hears the oboe resolve, etc.

In the final measure of the Largo, the thirty-second-note before the fermata should be heard the same length in time as the third note, the written sixteenth-note, in the beginning three measures, which in performance practice is now also heard as a thirty-second-note. To make the thirty-second-note in the final cadence crushed into the fermata, as if to dramatically set it off, would not be in the style.

The fermata over the half-note meant "end of the Largo" for Mozart and it probably should not be elongated beyond two beats. Here is the ideal place for an *Eingang,* a few notes to make a smooth transition to the next section. In practice it was usually played by the instrument which has the melody to begin the next section, as here by the first clarinet. But in this case we have a special circumstance in the fact that the new section is marked *piano*, which is unusual for the beginning of a Molto Allegro section.

But more important than just being *piano*, the new section begins with a special feature found in earlier dances. In some Baroque instrumental dance manuscripts one will see just such a brief introduction set apart from the actual beginning of the dance. This reflects some earlier tradition of these court dances whereby things began with a formal recognition, an introduction of the aristocratic dancers. If the reader is familiar with the American Square Dances one will recall that they also began with a special introduction formula in which the Caller would say "Now bow to your partner ... and bow to the lady across the way," which was then followed by the actual first dance.

In this case we imagine the dancer in the first measure steps forward with the left foot and then follows with the right foot. In the second measure, still facing forward, as he brings the left foot back it automatically results in a bow and the purpose of the grace note is to facilitate the movement backward and the bow. The second quarter-note represents the closing of the feet, the clicking of the heels (which is also the purpose of the final "bump" note in the traditional march). The "introduction" having been made, the Allegro proper begins. The fact that this introductory music appears again in the course of the movement only reflects Mozart's fondness of showing he can make music out of nothing.

So, the *Eingang* which the clarinetist must perform between the end of the Largo and the beginning of the Allegro is unusually challenging, for it must now not only prepare the listener for the transition from a loud fermata to a *piano*, but must try to take the listener from the drama of the Largo to a sophisticated and elegant court ball.

In the above discussion of Mozart's notation of *ritard.*, the reader has seen that the symbol *p* during the time of Mozart could also mean "slow," and not just "soft." Therefore the *p* for this "introduction" may mean a slower tempo and then the real Molto Allegro begins a new tempo. In other words this section could remain *forte,* but just slower, with the only change necessary being in the clarinet *Eingang* which would now need no dimenuendo.

Almost all Mozart first movements are notated in common time, but were expected to be conducted *alla breve.* To conduct in four creates the same effect as hammering nails into a board, whereas in *alla breve* the music takes flight. The proof that this must be conducted *alla breve* is found in the initial bar of the Molto Allegro where we see one of Mozart's favorite figures, a syncopation. But it is a syncopation only if the meter is *alla breve,* for if in common time there is no syncopation—everything is on the beat!

There are several things to mention about the ending of this movement. First, in the 22nd and 23rd measures from the end we see the small "grace notes" which are performed before the beat, and not on the beat, as Mozart has clearly drawn them. In the cadence beginning 21 measures from the end we see on the second and fourth beats the familiar appoggiatura notation which means playing four even sixteenth-notes but with an accent on the first note, which provides a distinct up-beat 'kick,' giving a kind of syncopated feeling.

Figure 17: Mozart, "Gran Partita," к. 361, movt 1, Molto Allegro.

Following this is a Coda filled with little surprises. Among the few extant contemporary reviews of Mozart's music one sees several times a critic commenting that Mozart's music was "exotic." For us that seems a strange word, but it was things like this unusual coda which caused these comments to be made. First four measures of very strongly accented quarter-notes, followed by nothing—a grand pause! Then one measure of the same figure but at a soft level, then one measure at a loud level including a fermata! All of this drama was to grab the listener's attention for what came next. We hear the initial measure of this movement in B♭ as we would expect. but in the following measure an F♯ flirts with the key of B♮. We are lost in an harmonic sea but Mozart soon rescues us.

The final cadence, the final six measures, requires special attention. First, it is in what I call macro meter, meaning two measures of *alla breve* become one measure of 4/2. It is very important that the conductor conducts this in a pattern of four beats in order for the final two measures to make sense in terms of pulse. The final two measures represent one measure of 4/2, which means the performance must make the composition appear to end on the first of these final three notes, just as in any 4/2 measure the first beat must be the strongest. Mozart is back again thinking of dance here and on this first of these three notes, which is the "end," we see the dancer bow. On the next beat he raises his body upright and on the final note he floats his arms off to the sides as if to say, "and there we have it." The final note Mozart notates as a half-note in order to make sure the players will play a quarter-note, following the rule that a quarter-note followed by rests in a measure must be played one-half its written value. To lengthen this note, on what we used to call a "feminine cadence" years ago, would create the impression of leaving things up in the air and that another downbeat was still needed in a following measure to really sound like "the end."

Second Movement, Menuetto

It had been a very long time since anyone in Vienna had actually danced a Minuet, maybe since the time of Louis xiv. The Minuet had become strictly a stylized instrumental form, as had many of the other Baroque dance forms which were no longer danced. At this time the Vienna composers were moving toward the faster style we associate with Beethoven in his scherzo third movements. One sees this expressed among other Vienna composers, as in the example by Josef Triebensee in a movement called "Minuet allegretto." Mozart, even as a child, demonstrated extraordinary skill in picking up by ear the idioms around him and therefore in this Partita he writes two Minuets, this one in the old style and the next one in the new style. From a conducting perspective this first one is in three, the next one is in four. Being in the older style, this first Minuet should not be too fast, but rather on the stately and elegant side.

The several places where we see Mozart actually write out the word *crescendo,* spreading the letters of the word over four measures is a hallmark of the new era arriving when the composer takes over the performance decisions from the performer.

Third Movement, Adagio

Long before band directors discovered the "Gran Partita," this movement was known among Mozart specialists for its depth of emotion. One early scholar wrote that this movement was the "crown" of the Partita and another said, "Yes, and the accents in bars 25 and 26 are the thorns in the crown!"

The most intense expression of the dark emotion in this movement is found in the filling of the large leaps which Mozart left for the players to express themselves. While this type of filling in of large intervals was nothing new at this time, it is the pain which seems to surround them here which gives this movement such anguish. Mozart provides a model for the performance in the second entrance of the first oboe, m. 10. He shows diatonic filling with an accent at the top. The style required is not a mathematically divided progression of what Mozart has written as 32nd-notes, but a slight lingering on the first note and then the rest to portray a cry. Mozart has also written here dots, meaning accents, under a slur, resembling portamento. In the style it is thought that in vocal music the singer should employ a kind of emotional pressing and blending the notes together[14] for the purpose of depicting this kind of emotional cry. This filling in should occur on each place there is a leaping upward interval and this becomes an almost unbearable emotion when these intervals overlap among oboe, clarinet and basset horn in the 11th and 12th measures before the end, mm. 35–36. In the 8th measure from the end this should also be done when the first oboe and first basset horn "cry" together resulting in a painful tritone at the top! One cannot emphasize enough how fundamental this is to the movement, yet one almost never hears a performance where the conductor and players have the courage to do this. To not add this filling in which creates these emotional utterances is to leave the leaps as an almost comic jack-in-the-box effect.

Finally, one wonders what circumstance had overcome Mozart to write such painful music? The first known performance was

[14] Elson, *Dictionary,* 208.

in March 1784 and while we know of several important people
in Mozart's life who died in 1782, which will be discussed
in the following chapter, we know of no such events in the
months before March of 1784. If I were to offer a speculation I
would point to the fact that Mozart's first son, Raimund, had
died as an infant about six months before this movement was
first performed.

Regarding performance practice in the Adagio, I would suggest
a *crescendo* and *diminuendo* in the first measure to give some life
to this triad. In the bass line which follows the style should be
heavy and with always a slightly heavier pulse on the sixteenth-
notes which fall on the beat, in spite of the fact that Mozart
always shows a slight accent on the second sixteenth-note.

The general *ritard.* which Mozart notates in the next to last
measure with a *piano* becomes a very lengthy and drawn out
ritard. in the final measure, with the appearance of the ***pp***.
The more one draws out this final figure, the more elegant
the cadence becomes and the greater the aid in allowing the
listener to release the accumulation of emotion which has taken
place in this movement.

Fourth Movement, Menuetto – Allegretto

This Menuetto is in the new faster style. One finds this new
style in all the Beethoven symphony menuetts, which he
renamed Scherzi in view of the fact that the minuet was no
longer practiced as a court dance in Vienna. In this new style,
Beethoven combines four measures of 3/4 meter into the
fundamental formal unit which previously was represented
by a single measure, a practice which we call "macro meter."
There is a great deal of Beethoven's music which uses these
groups of four, as well in the last generation of the eighteenth
century, including the music of Mozart. One reason for this
practice was for ease in reading, for, as in the example of the
Beethoven Scherzi, the four bars of 3/4 in the older style would

have otherwise become one measure of 12/8 which would appear very crowded on paper and required much more ink for all the extra ligatures. Finally, in the Scherzi of Beethoven there is no question that he expected four of the new measures to be grouped together and conducted in four beats for in the Ninth Symphony where he makes a brief change he writes on the manuscript score "to be conducted in three," and then soon back to "to be conducted in four."

Therefore in this second Menuetto by Mozart the conductor must create a visual meter pattern which looks exactly as if the music were in 4/4 as all of the music falls into groups of four measures, each conducted with one beat. There is, however, one very important detail, important because it reflects the actual music and therefore must be observed. Mozart in his melodic design always treats the fourth of the group of four measures as a cadence, not simply as a fourth beat. One can see this "cadence" quality of the fourth measure very clearly in the first Trio of this Menuetto. The conductor can feel exactly what Mozart felt and communicate it clearly for the players by making the ictus of the third measure simply bounce back counter-clockwise to the center of the body for the fourth ictus and not in an upward bounce as one would prepare a fourth ictus which would lead to the next downbeat of music which continued.

The second Trio of this Menuetto is a lovely memorial to a kind of music Mozart must have heard often in the streets of Vienna, the music of the peasant organ-grinder. In the second section the dots are little accents, not mere staccato. At the end of this second section in the final measure for the string bass, the second note is performed only for the repeat of this section but only the first note alone before the *da capo*. Notice here again in the melodic voices in this measure, oboe, basset horn and bassoon, Mozart writes a half-note in order to produce a quarter-note in performance (in fear the players might extend the end of the phrase).

Fifth Movement, Romance

When I was a doctoral student at the Catholic University of America I had the opportunity to study the notation of early music with the very distinguished scholar, Father Woolen. Among other things, he taught us to examine carefully the margins of the paper and not just the notes. Accordingly, when I first looked at the autograph manuscript of the beginning of the Romance my eye was drawn to a solitary ink circle on the lowest staff, where it looked like perhaps he was going to notate a whole-note for the string bass. But this, at the same time, seemed unlikely as Mozart had left this lowest staff blank throughout this manuscript. Then I realized that this "circle" was actually merely an ink blot from the previous page, thereby leading to my having the great honor of solving a decades old debate about the "Gran Partita."

The origin of this famous blot was thus. It was Mozart's custom, when he finished a major section of music, to count the number of measures and write that number at the end of the section. This was solely for the benefit of his copyist, who, if he found the part he was writing had the same number of measures, could assume it was correct. In this case Mozart made a mistake and wrote the number "24," but then, realizing his error, wrote over the "24" the correct number "16" in heavier ink. At that point, perhaps, his wife called him to dinner and Mozart closed the book causing the heavier wet ink of the lower part of the "6" to blot on the following page. This little blot proved that the next manuscript page, even if it were blank, always followed the last page of the Menuetto.

The significance of this was as follows. Earlier scholars had great difficulty believing that Mozart would write such a great masterpiece, with a duration of more than an hour, as a single composition for mere wind instruments. Consequently there was a long debate with many scholars believing this must have been two compositions, one in B♭ major and one in E♭ major, which had in the course of time been bound together as one manuscript. To arrange the seven movements into two separate partitas in B♭ and in E♭, it was necessary, as a matter of tradition regarding the order of movements, that the second Menuetto and the Romance belonged to two separate partitas. But my discovery of the origin and meaning of the ink blot forever ended this debate, for, as I noted above, it proved beyond any doubt that the page which contains the first page of the Romance had always followed the last page of the second Menuetto.

Turning to the music of the Romance, aside from pointing out that measure eight of the second section contains a written out *Eingang,* it is very important for the conductor to realize that the cadence of the first section contains a *p* which meant *ritard.* This becomes very important when the same cadence appears before the Allegretto, for it allows a slower Allegretto of about quarter-note = 80 which in turn allows the solo bassoons to still be musical and not sound like a noisy machine of some sort.

This same measure in the autograph score, the measure before the Allegretto, contains another discovery which I am credited for. I was apparently the first to notice a small "1" above this measure in Mozart's handwriting which indicates that this measure is not played when this section is repeated. Instead this cadence is left incomplete and hangs in the air creating a magical connection with the following coda.

The final measure of the Romance, as I have discussed in a previous chapter, has a notated *ritard.* with a final note performed as a quarter-note, not a half-note, following the rule of the day.

Sixth Movement, Theme and Variations

The fifth variation begins with a *forte* fermata with a *diminuendo* written as a "hair pin," which Mozart had to do because he did not leave himself enough room to write *diminuendo.* Except for the final two variations, the movement should be conducted in two beats per measure.

Most conductors conduct the fifth variation very slowly owing to the appearance of 32nd-notes in the accompaniment. But this can cause the true melodic material to die from lack of motion. To understand this movement the conductor needs to sing the oboe part, thinking like a singer, to find a proper tempo, c. quarter-note = 68. Then, at first, those thirty-second-notes underneath will sound too fast, but if one has the players add a little *crescendo* and *decrescendo* on each two groups they will sound musical. However, the final eight measures may have been intended as more meditative and possibly in fact a little slower, as in Italian this symbol, *pp*, can mean either softer or slower.

The final variation should be conducted with one beat per measure, but in a pattern of four. In the final cadence Mozart may have been thinking of the well-known Masonic "three knocks on the door," a figure which makes a strong appearance in the beginning of the next and final movement.

Seventh Movement, Finale, Molto Allegro

This is a Rondo form during which Mozart creates great interest in the subordinate sections. The first subordinate section is based on the three "Masonic knocks" which begin each section. The conductor should clearly mark the initial three knocks, heard four times in the first section, to prepare the little musical joke when Mozart delays the third "knock" in the beginning of the second section.

We hear the principal section for the second time and then another subordinate section. This one consists of four sections of great variety, beginning with a little competition from the opera house. A tenor begins, a forward and lusty solo answered by the soprano. Now when they are really ready to compete with each other, Mozart shuts them down by thumbing his nose at them.

After another statement of the principal section, I think we are indeed presented with a little operatic scene, perhaps inspired by the interest of the public in the growing drama of the Napoleonic wars. This subordinate section begins with a vamp, a genuine military cadence complete with the "roll-off" of the drums at the end of the four bars. This represents a young Austrian soldier who is attracted to the bright uniforms and the glamour of the military and he wants to join. But then suddenly he stops and the thought comes as a headache, with his hand to his forehead, to a downward chromatic line, as he remembers, "But no, I have a wife and children and soldiers get killed!" Then he snaps out of it, and resumes his marching. But the thought returns, now longer and more painful. You can almost hear him at the fermata crying "Oh!" What comes next is the battle, expressed as it had been in so many earlier Baroque instrumental compositions by the confusion and the running of feet and here with even the climbing of a ladder followed by more running.

Following this brief battle music, what we hear beginning with the 15th measure from the end is characteristic "Finale Music" which tells us that this little operatic scene has ended and also reminds us that Mozart gave the name "Finale" to this movement. Nine measure from the end the curtain begins to fall and we can be sure the crowd is cheering and yelling "Bravo!" during the final five bars!

Mozart's Partita, K. 388

HERE IS A MOZART COMPOSITION which has puzzled Mozart scholars for more than a century. It is not just a quality work, it is one of the very best of all Mozart's compositions, a work of great depth of feeling, yet there is no record of any commission, no early performance nor any reference in Mozart's correspondence.

It is tempting to think Mozart wrote this, his first great composition of his Vienna period, as an introduction of himself. But if so, it did not turn out that way. This composition had such a strong personal relationship with Mozart that it was a very rare score that he never sold, never gave it to his wind player friends nor included it with so many other manuscripts he sent to Johann Traeg to make and sell copies of. He kept it on his desk until he died. He later arranged it for strings, but in doing so he made almost no changes.

But why was it written for winds? Earlier scholars always assumed that any sort of chamber work for winds must have been for some light, outdoor entertainment. The year before, in 1781, Mozart had dashed off the traditional sounding partita for six amateur players, the K. 375, but the K. 388 is a world apart, more personal and more symphonic.

A 1781 Mozart letter to his father mentions work on a "nacht musique," which is otherwise unknown, and so early scholars assumed this к. 388 must be that piece. I was the first person to say in print that the quality of this work makes it impossible for it to be this little evening serenade, and the later publication by Tyson on the water marks of the paper Mozart used proved me correct. The paper was not available before 1782.

I believe it is possible to firmly date the composition of this work as April 1782. But to understand this, especially in view of its very personal depth in the first three movements, one must first stand back and consider Mozart's state of mind during the previous year.

The year 1781 for Mozart begins in Munich, where the premiere of his opera *Idomeneo*, к. 366, was given. This had to have been a wonderful experience for Mozart, because aside from the interest in him because of the opera, Munich was, and is, a wonderful city and in every way a greater cultural and cosmopolitan environment than Salzburg.

But in March 1781, the Archbishop Colloredo, Mozart's employer, is in Vienna for the ceremonies celebrating the accession of Joseph II to the Austrian throne. To play his role among the aristocrats in Vienna, Colloredo wants to be surrounded by his own staff so he ordered Mozart to leave Munich and come to Vienna. Because of his opera's success in Munich, and his widely known reputation as a child prodigy, Mozart's name was known among musicians in Vienna. But Colloredo treated Mozart as if he were a rare painting that he owned but never showed to anyone. He made Mozart join him in Vienna but then refused to make him available to aristocrats who wanted to meet him. Mozart had an offer from the Countess Thun to perform in her palace on an occasion when the Emperor would be present and for a very large fee. Colloredo would not let Mozart accept. Furthermore, Colloredo housed Mozart in a building together with his lowest servants. Colloredo's treatment was obvious and Mozart was understandably offended. In May Mozart asks to be relieved from his service under Colloredo and was refused. Then the following month Mozart asks Colloredo again to be set free, the Archbishop, deciding

to teach him a lesson and let him starve to death, releases
Mozart from his service and his dismissal was punctuated
when the archbishop's chamberlain, Count Arco, sent Mozart
out the door with a kick in the pants. Mozart was angered and
humiliated.

We must assume that during these months in Vienna that
Mozart, in spite of his growing frustration and anger, must
have been meeting and talking with influential musicians in
town, who were no doubt assuring him that he had a bright
future if only he came to Vienna to live and work. With his
youthful confidence, and judging by the music he was hearing
around him in Vienna, Mozart had no difficulty in deciding to
locate there as a freelance performer and composer.

Almost immediately after his arrival in Vienna, Mozart was
circulating among and making friends among the aristocrats.
He writes his father on 23 January 1782 that he already has
several interesting possibilities. One, he explains, was with the
emperor's brother, Maximilian.

> Now of him I can say that he thinks the world of me. He shoves
> me forward on every occasion, and I might almost say with
> certainty that if at this moment he were Elector of Köln, I should
> be his Kapellmeister.

Maximilian soon did receive the title of Elector of Köln and
almost immediately founded his own Harmoniemusik in
imitation of the one his brother founded in Vienna in April
1782. Had Mozart become the Kapellmeister for Maximilian's
court, he would have had among the members of his orchestra
the young Beethoven.

But for Mozart the more immediate opportunity seemed to lie
with one of the great princes of Vienna, Prince Liechtenstein.
Mozart, in this same letter, indicates some discussions had in
fact taken place.

Young Prince Liechtenstein, who would like to collect a wind-
instrument band (though he does not yet want it to be known),
for which I should write the music. This would not bring in very
much, it is true, but it would be at least something certain, and I
should not sign the contract unless it were to be for life.

Wind conductors today can only imagine the affect on our
profession if Mozart would have been writing wind music the
last ten years of his life! The element of secrecy involved here
was because the emperor himself was thinking about founding
a Harmoniemusik, made up of the principal players of his
opera orchestra, and naturally no other aristocrat could afford
to do this before the emperor did.

In fact, the emperor did organize his Harmoniemusik two
months later, in April 1782, the same month we associate with
the composition of the Partita, κ. 388. Mozart must have been
talking with these leading wind players, otherwise he would
not have heard about the rumor of Liechtenstein forming a
Harmoniemusik. But Mozart, as we know from this same letter,
was known to the emperor and felt some opportunity existed
there. Of his possible opportunities, he tells his father,

> The second (in my estimation, however, it is the first) is the
> Emperor himself. Who knows? I intend to talk to Herr von
> Strack about it and I am certain that he will do all he can, for
> he has proved to be a very good friend of mine; though indeed
> these court flunkeys are never to be trusted. The manner in
> which the Emperor has spoken to me has given me some hope.

We know the Emperor was well acquainted with Mozart's
skill as a keyboard player, for the previous December he had
arranged a competition between Mozart and Muzio Clementi
to play in his presence. Mozart must have done well on this
occasion for he writes his father on 12 January 1782,

> Clementi! plays well, so far as execution with the right hand
> goes. His greatest strength lies in his passages in thirds. Apart
> from this, he has not a kreutzer's worth of taste or feeling in
> short he is simply a mechanicus.

MOZART'S PARTITA, K. 388   69

Four days later, Mozart writes his father with further details of this interesting competition,

> After we had stood on ceremony long enough, the Emperor declared that Clementi ought to begin. "La Santa Chiesa Cattolica," he said, Clementi being a Roman. He improvised and then played a sonata. The Emperor then turned to me: "Allons, fire away." I improvised and played variations. The Grand Duchess produced some sonatas by Paisiello (wretchedly written out in his own hand), of which I had to play the Allegros and Clementi the Andantes and Rondos. We then selected a theme from them and developed it on two piano fortes. The funny thing was that although I had borrowed Countess Thun's pianoforte, I only played on it when I played alone; such was the Emperor's desire and, by the way, the other instrument was out of tune and three of the keys were stuck. "That doesn't matter," said the Emperor. Well, I put the best construction on it I could, that is, that the Emperor, already knowing my skill and my knowledge of music, was only desirous of showing especial courtesy to a foreigner. Besides, I have it from a very good source that he was extremely pleased with me. He was very gracious, said a great deal to me privately, and even mentioned my [prospective] marriage. Who knows? Perhaps what do you think?

One can imagine Mozart, having this kind of recognition from the emperor, must have had his hopes high that he would be taken into his permanent service, which would have assured his career in Vienna. By 18 April, he writes his father that he really believed this was imminent.

> I have said nothing to you about the rumor you mention of my being certainly taken into the Emperor's service, because I myself know nothing about it. It is true that here too the whole town is ringing with it and that a number of people have already congratulated me. I am quite ready to believe that it has been discussed with the Emperor and that perhaps he is contemplating it. But up to this moment I have no definite information. At all events things are so far advanced that the Emperor is considering it, and that too without my having taken a single step. I have been a few times to see Herr von Strack (who is certainly a very good friend of mine) in order

to let myself be seen and because I like his society, but I have
not gone often, because I do not wish to become a nuisance to
him, or to let him think that I have ulterior motives. As a man
of honor he is bound to state that he has never heard me say a
word which would give him reason to think that I should like
to stay in Vienna, let alone enter the Emperor's service. We
have only discussed music. Therefore it must have been quite
spontaneously and entirely without self-interest that he has
been speaking so favorably of me to the Emperor. If things have
gone so far without any effort on my part, they can now proceed
to their conclusion in the same way. For if one makes any move
oneself, one immediately receives less pay, because, as it is, the
Emperor is a niggard. If he wants me, he must pay me, for the
honor alone of serving him is not enough. Indeed, if he were to
offer me 1000 gulden and some Count 2000, I should decline
the former proposal with thanks and go to the Count that is, of
course, if it were a permanent arrangement.

After the angry confrontation with Archbishop Colloredo the
previous year, and waiting around in hope that the emperor
in Vienna would offer him a position, one can clearly see that
Mozart is feeling the stress. Defensively he says, "well—I
wouldn't take the offer anyway." By April he was clearly
anxious.

Adding to this stress was growing frustrations in his personal
life. He takes a room in a rooming house run by Madame
Cäcilie Weber, a relative of Carl Maria von Weber. Here he falls
in love with her daughter, Aloysia Weber, but she rejects his
advances. Next he turns his attention to her sister, Constanze, a
lovely and, contrary to her musicological reputation, talented
and educated young lady.

Upon his arrival in Vienna, Mozart was giving lessons to
support himself and one of his students was Barbara von
Auernhammer, a dilettante pianist of some ability. They played
duets together, appeared in public together and to Mozart's
naïve astonishment she fell in love with him.

> Well, I have told you how she plays, and also why she begged
> me to assist her. I am delighted to do people favors, provided

they do not plague me incessantly. But she is not content if I
spend a couple of hours with her every day. She wants me to
sit there the whole day long and, what is more, she tries to be
attractive. But, what is worse still, she is serieusement in love
with me! I thought at first it was a joke, but now I know it to
be a fact. When I perceived it for she took liberties with me for
example, she made me tender reproaches if I came somewhat
later than usual or could not stay so long, and more nonsense
of the same kind I was obliged, not to make a fool of the girl, to
tell her the truth very politely. But that was no use: she became
more loving than ever. In the end I was always very polite to
her except when she started her nonsense and then I was very
rude. Whereupon she took my hand and said: "Dear Mozart,
please don't be so cross. You may say what you like, I am really
very fond of you!" Throughout the town people are saying that
we are to be married, and they are very surprised at me, I mean,
that I have chosen such a face. She told me that when anything
of the kind was said to her, she always laughed at it; but I know
from a certain person that she confirmed the rumor, adding that
we would then travel together.

So, by April 1782, the letters of Mozart to his family are filled
with his very complicated position. He has this history of
relationship with young ladies, he is particularly concerned
with this relationship with the Webers, for he is in love with
Constanze and he still had no means of support other than
teaching and performing. It is no wonder the young man's
Partita in C Minor, K. 388, is so emotional and personal in
character, and for that matter, in a minor key.

I will give below the specific reasons why I date this work
as April 1782, but in general it seems to me that Mozart is
waiting around for the emperor to offer him something. The
emperor in fact established his Harmoniemusik in this month
and Mozart, with his friendships among the wind players
and his negotiations with Prince Liechtenstein regarding a
position leading his Harmoniemusik, must have thought that
a similar position was going to be offered by the emperor.
Preparing a high quality composition in advance for such
an opportunity would have been a natural thing to do. But
the emperor appointed his first oboe instead as the leader,

and there was no occasion for Mozart to present this partita. Mozart's association with this partita and his disappointment in this missing opportunity, together with all the feelings he had poured into this composition, may well explain why he laid it aside on his desk and could never bring himself to give it away.

First Movement, Allegro

This is the most unusual sonata form I know of by any composer before 1782. It is certainly not the Mozart of Salzburg. This is not an example of a composer who says this morning I will write the first movement and here is the theme. Certainly in terms of the definition of the sonata form as it was then understood at this time, as a form based on tonal centers, and not on themes, it meets its expectations.

But superseding all of the above, what we immediately feel here is a sense of turmoil, with starting and stopping, and it's almost angry character at the beginning and at m. 10 which is so startling. It is almost as if we feel we have arrived late and missed something important which had happened earlier. It would be almost forty measures before we hear something which sounds like a traditional melody and it turns out to be the second tonal area.

What has happened earlier, of course, and something from which Mozart has not yet freed his mind, was the humiliation of his clash with the archbishop and his personal abuse from a court official. This agitation remains and in the closing section Mozart provides us with an almost operatic scene which personifies his feelings.

But first, to return to matters of performance practice, like most Mozart first movements written in common time, this movement is clearly to be conducted in two and not in four beats. The conductor should find the tempo in the lyrical melody which begins in m. 42.

The ornament in m. 14 and following should be thought of only as accents at the *piano* level. In reality they can probably be little more than a mordant without sounding awkward. In m. 22 the conductor must be careful that the busy figuration does not prevent the listener from hearing the more important initial motive in the bassoons.

According to the practice in Vienna at the time, Mozart expected m. 39 to be performed as a quarter-note and it certainly should be. He also assumed, of course, that the second clarinet part beginning in m. 42 be entirely slurred.

The above is analysis of a very traditional nature, as is appropriate to the music. But for the closing section it is rather an analysis of the emotions which seems appropriate, as Mozart's thoughts return to the humiliation he still suffers from. The first measures of the closing section, mm. 67–73, sound like typical closing material but the *subito forte* gives it a stronger, dogmatic quality, which we take to represent the court officials angry utterance, "and don't forget it!" This is followed by a repetition, but at the *piano* level, as if the court employee is repeating this warning to show he understands it. Then in *forte* measures 79–81, the angry official again yells, "Don't forget it!" Two bars of *piano*, with an accent at the *piano* level follow, representing the employee suffering. Here in the autograph score Mozart circles this last exchange indicating it is to be repeated to further rub in the humiliation. Then the final closing measures beginning at m. 90 are *piano*, not the usual *forte* of a closing section. This represents the humble employee rapidly tip-toeing away and when out of range of the court official the employee has the last comment—some loud comments to himself in m. 93 with the final two quarter-notes marked with a marcato strong accent, a more obscene version of "Take that!"

The development section is again very unusual, with an almost improvisation sounding clarinet solo over the descending diatonic lines in the bassoon and second clarinet. There should be no tie in the first clarinet between mm. 101 and 102. Whatever Mozart was thinking in these measures, is followed in m. 107 by the placement idiom, which here is so important that Mozart writes it out to allow the previous material to drift off into space. It is certainly not necessary to add that this blank bar is not conducted.

This brief development section, with its fragmentation set apart by long pauses, seems to join the exposition section in giving an overall impression of the agitated state of mind in which Mozart found himself in April 1782.

Second Movement, Andante

As the second movement begins one feels Mozart must have exhausted his angry emotions in the first movement, or at least achieved some control of them, for this movement begins with a calm atmosphere and pleasing melody, almost the very picture of tranquility. It also has a moment of humor, a vigorous country dance complete with the dancer kicking out his leg.

It is at this point, toward the end of the exposition section and the beginning of the development section, however, that there may have been a pause in composition, for something has happened and the following music is miles apart from what Mozart has written to this point. In fact, it is because this development section is so different, so dramatic and personal that cause me to believe that this moment is one of the factors which I believe date this composition as being written in April 1782.

What has happened? On 23 March 1782, aside from the arrival in Vienna of the pope, the father of the girl who was in love with him, Herr von Auernhammer, died. Mozart liked him, calling him a good and kind man. Then on 10 April Mozart heard that Johann Christian Bach had died in London, causing Mozart to write his father saying, "What a loss for the Musical World!" On the first big tour to London, when Mozart was a child, Bach had treated them with greater cordiality and offered more help than any other host in any other city. Mozart had always retained a fond memory of Bach from that visit. Two days later, on 12 April, in Vienna, the poet Metastasio died. It was his work which had inspired the libretto of Mozart's *Idomeneo* which premiered the previous year in Munich. These last two deaths of people who meant a lot to Mozart, coming two days apart, must have given Mozart pause. For one with a long history of illness since childhood, and it now being one year after the death of his own first child, it is possible that Mozart was for the first time thinking of his own mortality. I personally think it would not be too far a leap to suggest that with the news of the death of Bach and Metastasio, on 10 and 12 April 1782, and its impact on Mozart, might well mark the moment when this Andante becomes so contemplative. Now it seems as if Mozart's attention is miles away. Three times he begins the first theme and leaves it hanging unfinished in space. The effect is haunting and sad. Even when he decides to begin the recapitulation he makes a mistake, creates a unique symbol changing a *da capo* to a *dal segno,* which tell us his mind still wasn't back in the present tense.

Regarding performance practice, in this haunting and melancholic development section, the three phrases of the development must be set off with Placement. One must recall that when the music stops, as also is the case after a fermata, the two eighth-notes rest no longer have a value. It is a perfect example of "Placement," meaning the conductor begins again only when he feels it is emotionally right and not on the basis of any aspect of time before. Three times this happens, leaving the listener, like Mozart, suspended in another world. Only the recapitulation brings us back to the present tense, listening to a composition.

Perhaps a few additional comments on performance practice in this movement are appropriate. First, the conductor must not allow the visual look of all the ligatures cause him to conclude that the tempo must be very slow. The ligatures are there only because the meter is 3/8. In the Classical Period the Andante was considered the slowest of the fast tempi and here I would recommend the eighth-note beat as being about eighth-note = 74.

I believe most early music specialists would agree that the ornament in m. 29 was intended to be a four-note turn, leaving two sixteenth-notes on the third beat. The question is, is the turn on the second beat or after the second beat. I prefer the more lyrical choice of placing it on the second beat. My experience, in either case, is that one should actually write the resolution out on paper for the student musician. A verbal explanation is too confusing, as the reader has just experienced.

Figure 18: Mozart, Partita к. 388, mm. 29–31, manuscript.

Figure 19: Mozart, Partita к. 388, m. 29, with applied performance practice.

The new music, the rollicking country dance at m. 32 should be faster; it is completely in the style to have such internal variety in tempo. Clearly, the country dancer kicking out his leg, as represented in the bassoons, would feel quite off-balance at a slower tempo. It is also clear that Mozart intended this because he so carefully creates the *ritard.* bar, m. 38, the *p* meaning slower, not softer, where three slowing steps return us to the original slower tempo and more tranquil closing section. The final two eighth-notes of the exposition section, mm. 45–46, are marked with a strong marcato accent in the autograph score, not as staccato seen in some editions.

These two strong marcato eighth-notes are not found at the end of the recapitulation, however. The haunting and contemplative development section and the strong emotions it creates changes everything. The listener still retains this experience and to end with these strong marcato eighth-notes would be like saying "I was just kidding!" Instead, they stay in the calm and contemplative mood and Mozart now adds *pp* which here means *ritard.* This change has these two final notes slowly drifting away in space, allowing a moment for the listener, and players, to release their emotions before the shocking beginning of the next movement.

Third Movement, Minuetto in Canone

Although I know of no writer who has mentioned it, I believe this Minuet is a hallmark of the fact that Mozart's anger and frustration with the archbishop is still with him. It is perfectly normal and human. The Minuet has not been danced much in court since the period of Louis xiv in France. By the late eighteenth century it had become purely the name of an instrumental dance and a rather simple and homely one at that. It was, then, no subtle gesture when Mozart took the sacred styles of Church music, counterpoint and fugue, and cast them into the frame of a minuet. Furthermore, the fact that that must have been associated with the archbishop is evident in the pure anger expressed in the beginning measures. This interpretation is further made clear in the following section, where Mozart, in the most innocent and humble sounding music, at a soft level, seems to say, "Who me? I meant no such thing," until jolts of emotion quickly drive him back to the angry counterpoint! The Trio, in another satire of the complicated Church style, is a simple two-part fugue, but with an inverted subject serving as a counter subject.

It is impossible to know the sequence of these events in Mozart's life, but it is clear he had not previously shown much interest in this contrapuntal style and now seemed to suddenly have an interest in the technique. Again, regarding the date of this composition, it is this sudden interest which caused him on 10 April 1782 to write his father,

> I have been intending to ask you, when you return the rondo, to enclose with it Handel's six fugues and Eberlin's toccatas and fugues. I go every Sunday at twelve o'clock to Baron van Swieten where nothing is played but Handel and Bach. I am collecting at the moment the fugues of Bach not only of Sebastian, but also of Emanuel and Friedemann. I am also collecting Handel's and should like to have the six I mentioned.

And ten days later, he writes his sister,

> Baron van Swieten, to whom I go every Sunday, gave me all the works of Handel and Sebastian Bach to take home with me (after I had played them to him). When Constanze heard the fugues, she absolutely fell in love with them. Now she will listen to nothing but fugues, and particularly (in this kind of composition) the works of Handel and Bach. Well, as she had often heard me play fugues out of my head, she asked me if I had ever written any down, and when I said I had not, she scolded me roundly for not recording some of my compositions in this most artistic and beautiful of all musical forms, and never ceased to entreat me until I wrote down a fugue for her.

Finally, there is another possibility that the sense of the music taking flight in the Trio might have been a residual echo of the rigid life under Archbishop Colloredo versus Mozart's present freedom? This, in turn, may reflect a more remote possibility. We don't hear much about it in this country, but the success of the American Revolution had an enormous influence on the people of Europe. For five years as the battle raged on, no one in Europe thought the American farmers could defeat the mighty British Empire. But when they did, suddenly the idea of ordinary people throwing off the chains of the monarchy which existed in every country started everyone thinking and was the topic of wide conversation. The contribution to the French Revolution is an obvious example. The actual end of the American Revolution came with the surrender of Cornwallis at Yorktown on 19 October 1781. News traveled slowly in the eighteenth century and judging by the four months it took before Mozart heard of the death of Johann Christian Bach in London, then it might have been only a few weeks before April 1782 when this news of the end of the war reached Mozart. Perhaps the background of this widespread celebration felt in Europe on the idea of being free may have contributed to the sense of freedom one senses in this Trio.

Fourth Movement, Allegro

The final movement, a very interesting set of variations, is much lighter in character, which is not unusual for final movements of the Classical Period. However, in the first section it is very possible that Mozart was still thinking about his poor treatment by the archbishop. This section, like some scene in a comic opera of the period, features a pompous aristocratic authority figure strutting around on the stage and bellowing out his own introduction. When I hear this melody I cannot help thinking it should have these words:

> "I am the migh–ty arch–bish–op and all must bow to me. My word is al–ways fin–al law,—but some–times I'm not sure."

This last phrase is in the first ending and the music conveys real self doubt, in contrast to the pompous beginning. Since in the performance of this partita neither the actor nor his words are present, it offers an interesting challenge for instrumentalists to convey the emotions of the scene. With a bit of introduction, the players have no difficulty sounding pompous, but how do they express the doubt in the first ending? When I conduct this work I explain to the players that they must convey this doubt individually in any way they can or wish, through body language while they play, or facial expressions or in their tone quality. The result is always immediate and amazingly effective.

The following variations are all very interesting. They include a rowdy country dance at m. 17, and a soft mysterious episode at m. 48. Of particular interest is m. 96 where the horns suddenly announce a fanfare that doesn't go anywhere, repeated by *piano* clarinets, trying to sound like distant horn players. What this leads to is a contest between the first and second oboes. Vienna at this time was filled with exceptional oboists and among the best were the two oboists in the emperor's opera company, Georg Triebensee and Johann Wendt. Here we hear one play eight measures followed by the other playing the same music. As they were evidently attempting to show off their musicianship, I always encourage student oboe players to freely move their bodies as they play so the audience will recognize the contest.

The final variation, beginning at m. 175, is very special. The variation at m. 175 is *pianissimo* throughout, with little, tiny accents. With all its harmonic surprises it is the kind of passage which local critics called "exotic." It concludes with a fermata, a written out placement idiom where the first oboe must perform an *Eingang* to set up the coming surprise, a C major ending to a C minor Partita, as well as a return to the *forte* level. In the later transcription of this partita which Mozart scored for strings, he wrote out this *Eingang*.

This later string version also comes to our rescue in knowing how the original partita for winds ended, for the final page of the autograph score is missing! The first published score, by Breitkopf & Härtel in 1880, has an error by which it gives no third in the final chord. It is not easy to hear because of the speed and volume, but the partita was for decades concluded without a third. Over the years I pointed this out and one conductor responded by contending that he believed Mozart wanted to end the work with a Medieval flavor!

Part III

THE STYLISTIC PRINCIPLES OF TRADITIONAL PERFORMANCE

Time and Music

TIME DOES NOT EXIST, say some philosophers. And they are right if we mean by Time an independent physical reality. Every concept we use to describe Time is a concept we made up—how long is a second, how long is a year, etc. We have attempted to find reality by assigning the length of a day and year to the rotation of our own planet. But all that is still something we made up and is information no longer useful when we refer to the planet Mars, where using the same basis for calculation a day is longer than a year.

Philosophers all agree that whatever we call Time is, it is linear, "the arrow of Time," and that we can acknowledge the idea of a past, present and future Time, but we are always only in the present tense and can only contemplate past and future Time from our present tense perspective.

Beyond this, philosophers have enormous difficulty explaining our perception of Time. St. Augustine (354–430 AD) began his discussion[15] with his famous question, "How can we say an interval of Time is long or short, when what is past can have no property such as 'long,' and neither can the present tense be described as long or short, as the present tense has no duration?" More recent philosophers raise such questions as, "Can we even experience the present tense when anything we perceive with our senses instantly becomes past tense?"

[15] *Confessions*, Book XI.

The fundamental reason why past philosophers have had such difficulty in discussing such questions is that they have been attempting to describe matters of the experiential side of ourselves in the language and linear thought process of the left-hemisphere of the brain; they were writing before the clinical discoveries which have confirmed our twin, bicameral beings. Our experiential understanding of Time lies in the right-hemisphere of the brain and it is real and independent of the left-hemisphere, where all our language, rational thought processes and books lie.

Therefore, while the left-hemisphere says, "No, the present tense has no duration," it is only speaking of Time in the observable changes in events in time by which present and past can be measured. But, in the right-hemisphere the present tense can have significant experiential duration for when one is listening to music the listener becomes the music and perceives the music and himself as being one in the present tense for so long as the music lasts. When the music stops, the listener and the musicians are at that moment in the present tense as well. During the music the musicians and the listener were experiencing together an extended present tense and it is irrelevant that their present tense differed with the rest of the world, for the rest of the world has continued to experience their own present tense as their lives progressed and in both cases this made-up word "present tense" must always have only a personal definition.

The philosopher who says "Time does not exist" is speaking of its description in left-hemisphere rational language. But in the right-hemisphere when we are performing or listening to music we are not experiencing Time itself, but rather a succession of experiences which have their only reality in matters of personal feeling for which the word, "Time," seems entirely inappropriate. One illustration of these entirely separate sets of perception can be seen in the example if one were reading a novel and at the end read, "Go back and read the first five chapters." This would make no sense to the linear left-hemisphere which read the book, but in the right-hemisphere we find pleasant feelings in recapitulations and *da capos*, seeing a long unseen friend or a long unvisited town. We see here proof of the validity of the recognition of the past tense in the right-hemisphere, an experiential past tense. Furthermore a sounding dominant seventh chord enables the right-hemisphere to predict the future, whereas the left-hemisphere has no such natural capacity.

Another interesting characteristic of the right-hemisphere's perception of music is that it does not seem to matter if we are listening to music which moves through time slowly or music which moves very fast, for in both cases we seem completely at one with the music though we ourselves are not moving. This, in the language of philosophers who write of Time, is called Empathy. It is this assumed empathy upon which Monteverdi placed his confidence when he told a singer who asked about the correct tempo, that it should be sung to the time of the heart, not the time of the hand. And it was this same meaning which Beethoven had in mind, when observing that the newly invented metronome was of value for only the first couple of measures, and "after that, feeling has its own tempo." And it was this same dependence on empathy behind the advice given from three famous eighteenth-century musicians on the question of tempo.

Joachim Quantz—It is necessary to take the tempo more from the content of the piece than from the [Italian] word at the top.[16]

* * *

K. P. E. Bach—The tempo of a piece ... is derived from its general mood together with the fastest notes and passages which it includes.[17]

* * *

Leopold Mozart—Tempo must be inferred from the music itself, and this is what infallibly shows the true quality of a musician.[18]

[16] *Essay on Flute Playing*, Berlin, 1752, XII, 2.

[17] *Essay on Keyboard Playing*, Berlin, 1753, III, 10.

[18] *Violinschule*, Augsburg, 1756, I, iii, 7.

To return to the question of Time, would an ancient man, walking along a path in the forest while playing his flute, have had a musical experience much different than a modern flute player walking alone down such a path? Except for the fact that the modern player did not make his own flute, probably not. Both players would have felt that they and their music were one experience in time, as both would have had the same goal of expressing their feeling through their music. Both would have been aware of the distinction between playing slow or fast and, both would have had some degree of awareness of pulse in their playing, especially when they were walking while playing. However, neither would likely have felt any need for what we think of today as Tempo, an artificial Time construction intended to govern how they played. For the musician today who is thinking about how to interpret a melody, I believe it is an invaluable prerequisite to contemplate how many centuries have passed during which music consisted of a one-line melody, including centuries of minstrels, early church music, the first man who sang in a shower and when my high school friends and I danced and sang the "Hokey Pokey" ("Put your left foot in, put your left foot out ..."). What is important for the musician today to remember is that given these eons of time during which civilization in all venues expressed its feeling in single melodic lines, one must imagine how careful and important the interpretation of melody must have evolved.

When, then, did Tempo become important to music making? Dance is surely the key, but one must remember that early couples or groups dancing knew meter, but not necessarily Tempo as we use the term today. Julius Pollux (2nd century AD) wrote of three kinds of dances: grave, gay and the third being some kind of combination of the first two. It should be no surprise that he describes these dances in emotional language, but not specifically in terms of Tempo. The theorist, Jean de Muris, writing in 1350, wrote that there were three speeds in music: quick, slow and medium, but this tells us little about the music. But in 1588 Thoinot Arbeau, in his *Orchesography,* gave the titles of three basse danses as "Comfort," "All Forlorn" and "Patience."

It is only with the courtly basse danse of the fifteenth century that the confluence of emotional expression, speed of dance and meter necessitated the additional element of precision of tempo, because as basse danse was a generic name for a number of dances known to the fifteenth-century aristocratic dancers by title and a mistake in Tempo or meter by the musicians would embarrass the dancers. They danced to a known tune played in the bass by a slide-trumpet. The other two accompanying instrumental voices, oboes, performed fast and complex improvisation, thereby leaving us most disappointed in the fact that the most interesting music of the fifteenth century was never written down and preserved. Generally, as reflected in the title, these dances were slow (basse = low to the floor), and, as Arbeau pointed out were, "dignified and well suited to honorable persons."

Thoinot Arbeau (1519–1595) lived after the great period of the aristocratic basse danse, although it was in the sixteenth century now danced by the public, but it is clear in his famous book on dancing, *Orchesography,* that the emphasis on character carried over to what we now know as the instrumental dances of the Baroque Period. It is for Arbeau's careful discussion of meter, speed, character and deportment of the dancers that makes his book so important. He specified, for example, that the Pavan was too solemn and slow to dance alone with a young girl in a room. He also adds that anyone who objects to this discussion of dancing "deserves to be fed upon goat's meat cooked in a pie without bacon!"

We also should point out that the instrumental form of these dances spread very widely, even in publications, during the Baroque Period. The seventeenth century, then, was really the first time that musicians became interested in playing and hearing earlier music. We might assume that the general styles of these pavans, sarabands and minuets gained a certain famil-iarity, for there is the curious evidence found in Beethoven's

Piano Sonata, op. 54, of 1804, where we find, as a tempo designation at the beginning of the first movement, "in Tempo d'un
Menuetto," even though this movement is not a minuet at all!

Tempo was an obvious component of military marching, which
was reintroduced to Europe during the Baroque by General
Maurice de Saxe (1696–1750). He received much criticism
from his troops when he forced them to learn to march in
coordinated steps, but he had observed that these same men
could dance all night without complaint. Because of him the
concept of standing armies, and with them established military
bands, became important.

Willi Apel points out that it was also during the Baroque that
the use of the familiar Italian words became a standard part of
notation,[19] pointing to Adriano Banchieri (1567–1634) and his
Organo suonarino of 1611 as one of the early examples. Michael
Praetorius[20] wrote in 1619 that it was probably a good idea for
composers to adopt this new practice.

But even as this long development of instrumental dance music
developed into strong traditions of pulse and tempo, there was
in consequence a musically unfortunate result. Once one began
to think of melody as music which filled the space between two
bar-lines, something was lost in the centuries old tradition of a
free melodic voice. The bar-line became a barrier to musicality,
a fact against which musicians suffer to the present day.

The result of this struggle against the tyranny of the bar-
line resulted in a new practice in early music performance
in which, especially in internal cadences, the solo player
would take whatever time seemed appropriate and the other
players simply waited until it felt musically the "right time"
to continue. Early music specialists call this "Placement,"
meaning to place the beginning after a rest not according to
chronological time but according to experiential time—when
it feels right to begin again. The creation of this moment for
musical freedom was caused therefore by simply stopping, for

[19] *Harvard Dictionary of Music,* 1953, 737.

[20] *Syntagma musicum,* III, 51.

once Time stops the remaining rests in the measure have no meaning at all in the mathematical measurement of Time.

The great impetus for this new experience in which the musician controlled the Time within the measure came from the beginning of opera in 1600. The idea of opera was to use music to create a more vivid emotional experience than found in traditional stage plays using only the spoken voice. The form which we find at the beginning of opera is one in which the composer writes the most simple musical fragment, based on the words of the story involved and then the singer would take this material and make it dramatic by using his own improvisation to supply the emotions which words themselves cannot supply. As in the case of the basse danse, we are again left with extant material which does not include the improvisation, which was the most and only musical element involved. I have actually heard a university performance of one of these early operas which consisted of only the composer's fragmentary outline. Everything musical was missing and the result was a meaningless bore. This practice, but with the solo part now mostly written out, would become the recitatives of nineteenth-century opera.

This musical freedom created by the musicians taking over the Time between the bar-lines was not lost on Mozart. He created more flexibility within the concept of meter and Time than any composer before Schubert and Beethoven. A frequent example in Mozart is the *Eingang,* a term actually invented by Mozart himself, for a practice which also appears in the late Baroque Period. The *Eingänge* are brief, written out or unwritten, passages in a solo instrument for the purpose of bridging one section to another, something Mozart was particularly concerned about. *Eingänge* are classified as places for improvisation, and were generally brief with the fermata over a dominant or substitute dominant chord. The Cadenza, on the other hand, another important place for improvisation, has the fermata over a second inversion tonic chord, usually near the end of a movement, and during the Classical Period were quite lengthy, usually about 10% of the length of the movement. It is very important for students to learn the difference between these two kinds of fermata. Some clarinetists, for example, play cadenzas in the Mozart Clarinet Concerto, where in fact there are none—only *Eingänge*.

Another interesting example of Mozart's suspension of Time is found in the Andante movement of his Partita in C Minor for wind instruments, K. 388, which we have discussed earlier.

Another reorganization of Time, in a larger sense, is when one finds during the Classical Period what we call macro-meter, cases, for example, where perhaps four measures taken together form one measure musically. The third movements, the Scherzi, of the Beethoven symphonies is such an example. They are notated in 3/4 but conducted as if groups of four measures formed one large measure, sounding to the listener who did not have a score as if the music were in the meter 12/8. Why did Beethoven not write the music in 12/8 to begin with? The answer is that so many extra ligatures would become necessary that the music would be very difficult to read at a fast tempo. There is no question that Beethoven had this larger metric unit in mind because when you get to the Ninth Symphony scherzo, in m. 177 he writes a note for the conductor, "Ritmo di tre Battute," or conduct in three. In m. 234 he writes, "Ritmo di quattro Battute," conduct in four, as we presume the beginning was. To demonstrate how important this is, there was a long debate during the nineteenth century whether the Beethoven Fifth Symphony began with a down-beat or an up-beat, the conductors all assuming (correctly) that the music was too fast to be conducted in the meter it was written, 2/4. There was no universal agreement until Felix Weingartner pointed out that it must be conducted as if four measures formed a musically logical pattern. This is quite clear in the final measures before the repeat of the exposition section, where we discover the composition began on a "4th beat."

This principle has many important implications for interpreta-tion, even in the music of Mozart. In the "Gran Partita," K. 361, for example, there are two Minuets, but they are quite different. One represents an old-style minuet, which one conducts in three beats per measure, but the other is a new-style minuet which, like Beethoven scherzi, must be conducted in four in order to make the music logical.

For many important composers, the nineteenth century carried the revolt against a rigid concept of Time even further. One only has to think of the extensive use of *rubato* ("stolen time" in Italian) for expressive purposes in the music of Chopin to understand how strong was the undercurrent against the formalism of the Classical Period. Chopin, by the way, coined a nice analogy regarding the relationship of Time and rubato: the trunk of a tree from which branches and leaves are in constant motion.

In the case of Debussy one can see the sense of rebellion against Classical formalism in his seeking new kinds of harmony. Wagner in particular sought to end the barrier of the bar-line by composing what he called "endless melody." One wit at the time said, "No, Mozart is endless melody, your music is endless recitative!"

Debussy, Wagner and all the so-called Romantic composers of the nineteenth century came full-circle back to what musicians must have felt when notation first appeared in the Middle Ages, that is that no left-hemisphere written language can ever express the feelings of the present tense, experiential right-hemisphere—the artist as a real person. And they were right, those symbols on paper were never the real thing, only just symbols of the real thing. The point of view of performers then has become a duty to communicate the "real thing," and not just the notes on paper.

The purpose of music is to communicate feelings to the listener and nothing documents this more clearly than how the wide public which was drawn to serious music at the end of the nineteenth century. But anything which attracts the wide public carries the seeds of decay, a principle which can be seen over and over again since the period of the ancient Greeks. When applause becomes the goal, quality will always give way to the call of the masses for entertainment. Music education has thus far been unable to stem this tide.

The twentieth century, emotionally depleted by a great depression and two world wars, was left with an academic aesthetic which said, "just play what is on the page." But there is no music on the page, only the grammar of a musical language, something only the academics were interested in, leaving the broad public with nowhere else to turn but entertainment music. The relatively high level of entertainment music at the beginning of the twentieth century, represented by Irving Berlin, Sousa, Joplin and Gershwin, was soon subject to the same applause-driven principle mentioned above. The decline soon reached the level of rock and roll and it continues today, still seeking the bottom.

How does a Composer stop Time?

FOR A MILLION YEARS OR MORE, singers and instrumentalists playing on natural instruments made music freely with the sole goal of expressing their feelings. But once notation appeared the "rules" of music began to be addressed to the eye rather than the ear. The creation of bar lines in the eleventh century created units of time itself which lent to the eye the apparent rule that music must be contained within these units and the freedom of the ancient musicians was now lost for good. The subsequent history of notation was a constant effort to allow an escape from these preset units of time, including such things as colored notation and proportional notation. By the time of the Baroque, composers such as Praetorius and Frescabaldi began to write "just ignore the notation; play faster or slower as you desire." And by the eighteenth century it is amazing to see the lengths composers such as Haydn went to to write music that fell between those bar lines, but sounded as if it were in an entirely different meter or tempo. By the advent of music schools in the nineteenth century a new rigidity became the rule and as a result today no student believes he is entitled to expand a measure of music in performance solely on the basis of his feelings.

All notation is essentially an anti-musical construction and we must believe that all musicians have always rebelled against restriction to limit their expression. Thus we find even before the modern notational system, during the period of neume notation, the monk Notker of St. Gall (840–912), discusses in one of his letters the use of the letter "t" in plainsong notation to mean "trahere vel tenere debere," suggesting the stretching of the music to express the feeling of the words. We cannot call this the first use of *tenuto* because in his discussion it is evident someone else was already doing this.

The fermata symbol, which appears as early as the fifteenth century in the music of Dufay, is another vestige of the fight against legislated time in music. Most of us, when young musicians, were told that the familiar fermata "bird's eye" symbol ⌢ meant only a "stopping place." And so it does today for ordinary citizens living in Milan, for the symbol appears on all bus stop signs. But this symbol can mean many other things in music notation. Mozart used it, for example, over the final double bar of a composition to make sure the copyist understood this was really the end of the composition. He also used it to signify both cadenzas and *Eingänge* points, the difference being a matter of harmony. Bach, in his chorales, used it to designate where the singers breathe.

An alternative definition of fermata is to pause, but not stop. An example is found near the end of the final Rondo in Mozart's "Gran Partita," K. 361. The music, to the confusion of many conductors, just seems to hesitate, without a break in the progression of the music. In my experience, such a use of the fermata symbol associated with a pause seems to have an emotional connection, which is certainly relevant to my understanding in the Mozart example.

This use of the fermata symbol to create pause for an emotional reason is perfectly illustrated in the beginning of the Sixth Symphony of Beethoven. Here I must pause to remind those friends who have shared with me the mild winters of California and Texas that all of Europe is further North than our State of Maine. Having lived for three years in Vienna and Salzburg, I can understand the great experience of that day which arrives suddenly announcing Spring. The return of Spring was the most familiar subject, after love, of the Troubadours in their numerous original songs.

And it was from this background of the joy of the sudden return of Spring, the return of color and the return of birds that Beethoven, in the very beginning of the symphony, runs from his house and in the fourth bar immediately stops, in awe of the beauty of Nature, takes a deep breath of the fresh new air and then continues on his way. That is what the fermata here is all about, a pause, not a stop, to express feeling. The note he wrote here, "Awakening of cheerful feelings upon arrival in the countryside" clearly includes his emotion, as did his often quoted description of the entire symphony, "more an expression of feeling than painting."

As in the practice of the fermata, the current literal meaning of *tenuto* in Italian speech and in music has to do with holding on to something. I have begun to think that in the early nineteenth century the implied elongation by the word *tenuto* was tied to feeling and was not yet thought of as an articulation. In such a use it would be very similar to the Beethoven Sixth Symphony example mentioned above. I have been working on a modern edition of a Requiem for chorus and band which was commissioned, in a highly charged emotional atmosphere, for the reburial of Louis xvi on 21 January 1815 in Paris. In the first movement, a Marche funèbre, the internal cadences of the melody are marked *tenu*. There is no logic here for an accent, but when I sing this and elongate the measure one immediately feels a much stronger emotional expression.

This association of elongation for the communication of feeling seems to me exactly what is implied in Beethoven's little masterpiece, his Andante for wind instruments. Here again, in the internal cadences, he writes "ten" and by elongating this note, and the notes leading into it, the result is a much more expressive feeling. It is particularly enlightening that at the end of this composition when two unaccompanied horns are representing the court persons riding off into the distance, Beethoven still writes "ten" even though he also writes "senza

tempo." That is, the feeling he associated with the cadence and
its elongation is maintained even though it no longer has any
association with tempo. As a natural result of this association
between elongation and feeling, Beethoven concludes with an
augmentation of his initial melodic material, a very touching
and poignant ending.

After Beethoven, one finds in the highly idiosyncratic music
of Chopin uses of *tenuto* which are very puzzling and gives
one the feeling that it would be only in hearing Chopin himself
play that we would understand what he meant. What, for
example, was he thinking in his Scherzo, op. 39, no. 3, when he
wrote three bars of tied G♯, mm. 33–35, with "ten." over the
beginning of the first bar? Under the second bar is a *diminuendo*
sign and a *piano* symbol, appearing to represent the natural
decay of a long sound struck on the piano. But what did he
expect *tenuto* would add to this?

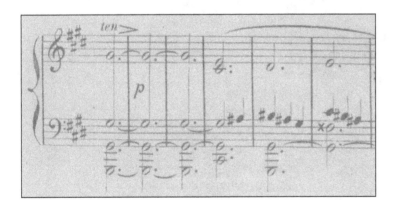

Figure 20: Chopin, Scherzo, op. 39, no. 3,
mm. 33–38

Similarily, in his Barcarolle, op. 60, in m. 39 one finds *tenuto* over the beginning of a tone lasting seven beats, also with a *diminuendo* beneath leading to *sotto voce*. Again, what could *tenuto* add to this?

Figure 21: Chopin, Barcarolle, op. 60, mm. 39–41

In his Polonaise, op. 26, no. 1, in mm. 8 and 20 there is *tenuto* written over a bar which looks as if it were part of a cadence which might sound expressive as a *ritenuto,* but since in both cases he writes "*ritenuto*" two bars later we have to assume that he would have used this word if that is what he meant. So, what did *tenuto* mean here?[21]

[21] Especially interesting here is the use of *tenuto* ("to hold" in Italian) and two bars later *ritenuto* ("reserved, self-possessed, retained, kept-back" in Italian).

Figure 22: Chopin, Polonaise, op. 26, no. 1, mm. 8–10

In the Nocturne, op. 27, no. 1, at the Più mosso, in the meter of 3/4 we find four bars of a melodic figure consisting of a dotted quarter-note followed by an eighth-note and a quarter-note, with *tenuto* written over each of the dotted quarter-notes. Five bars later this figure appears as double dotted, now a double dotted quarter-note followed by a sixteenth-note, etc., but no *tenuto* marking. So does *tenuto* here mean a holding back of the dotted quarter-note to become something longer, but not as long as being double dotted?

It is in this same Nocturne, beginning in the third bar, that we see, I believe for the first time in Chopin, the more familiar notation of quarter-notes which have both dots over the note heads and a slur over groups of such notes. This is the appearance which most musicians today would probably call *tenuto*.

Beginning by about the middle of the nineteenth century pianists become the first to speak of the *tenuto* symbol as meaning an accent. J. Frank Leve, a publisher of materials for the piano during the early years of the twentieth century, writes,[22]

[22] *The Etude* magazine, vol. 32, p. 567.

> I have adopted the sign (–) as a pressure sign because in classical works where this sign is used it is best produced by the pressure touch, notwithstanding in musical dictionaries it is defined as *tenuto,* sustained. My claim is that the sign (–) does not mean *tenuto* in the same sense as when the musical term is used. It rather means, in addition to the note being held for the full time, that it is produced by a pressure on the key.

He then quotes the famous pianist, Josef Hofman (1876–1957), as adding,

> It means that the notes should be played in such a way as to stand somewhat isolated from each other and held down, but not long enough to form a legato. It also implies a certain emphasis.

The use of the word emphasis here by Hofman, documents the arrival of the impression that some have today that the *tenuto* is in fact a kind of accent. We can see this again in a comment on the *tenuto* by Arnold Dolmetsch (1858–1940), in an online article,[23]

[23] https://bit.ly/3MV7eC1

> Tenuto can mean either hold the note in question its full length (or longer, with slight rubato) or else play the note

slightly louder. In other words, the tenuto mark is sometimes interpreted as an articulation mark and sometimes as a dynamic mark.

This brings us to an observation by Siglind Bruhn (b. 1951) in Germany, who, in her *Guidelines to Piano Interpretation*,[24] calls the *tenuto* "the most abrupt of all agogic processes." Going further, she writes, "a tenuto applied wisely comes unexpectedly and causes surprise." That is a long way from the emotionally expressive use by Beethoven.

[24] p. 49

How do we find the Tempo?

FOR MANY CONDUCTORS, tempo begins with that Italian word in the upper left corner of the music page. This tradition began in the early years of the seventeenth century and was intended to communicate character, as for example "Grave," rather than tempo. By the second half of the century, Johann Mattheson reports that Allegro means comfort and that Andante means hope! Most conductors will be surprised at this and that is because, as Leopold Mozart reports in 1756 in his famous book on violin playing, the Italian terms had already lost their meaning. That being the case, he recommended that performers should ignore them and instead discover the tempo of a composition through the study of the music itself, giving some helpful suggestions on how to do this.

In spite of the ubiquitous metronome, with actual numbers assigned to these Italian terms, as Leopold Mozart pointed out in 1756, these terms have no true meaning. Nevertheless, if you hand a new score to a young conducting student, the first thing he will do is look to see what is written in the upper left corner. If he sees Allegro, as an example, he immediately makes sweeping judgments about the composition, although he has yet to even glance at the actual music. How have we come to place so much importance on something which had already lost its meaning in 1756?

During the countless centuries of music history before notation, tempo must have been a subject of concern only with regard to dance music. All other solo performances would no doubt have always consisted of performance dictated by feeling. One can imagine that feeling also determined even dance tempi until such time as there were known and repeatable dances which would have tended toward a narrow range of recognizable tempi.

We have no way of knowing much about tempo with respect to the medieval two- and three-part scores, that is in the sense of individual performances. But, given the Church's role in turning music into a branch of mathematics, it would seem reasonable to guess that the notation did not anticipate internal tempo changes, such as *rubato,* no matter how much "feeling" the clerical singers were attempting to add to the music. In fact we may suppose it was their frustration in trying to be musical in a rigid mathematical system which led to the extensive improvisation in church music.

This aspect of tempo must have become even more problematic in Renaissance church music as it became notated for four, five and more parts. Certainly with proportions, in which the music rapidly became, through diminution, faster (smaller note values), the very mathematical complexity must have made tempo as we use the term irrelevant after the beginning. In some extant examples there quickly accumulate so many ligatures that it seems impossible to believe anyone could have actually sung the music. Some therefore consider these to be mere "educational examples" of the mathematics in question and not intended to be sung. But some music of this kind was sung and it was a real concern for working church music directors like Michael Praetorius in the sixteenth century. He feared the conductor might end up beating so fast that,

> we make the spectators laugh and offend the listeners with incessant hand and arm movements and give the crowd an opportunity for raillery and mockery.[25]

[25] *Syntagma Musicum,* III, 74. A facsimile of the original German publication has been printed by Bärenreiter Kassel, 1958. The page numbers we cite, therefore, are from the original print.

We suspect, therefore, that because of the notation itself, together with the Church background of making music be an expression of mathematics, rather than of emotion, that for most of the Renaissance performers probably no longer thought of tempo as an expression of feeling.[26]

[26] Please do not read this as meaning that Renaissance music was devoid of feeling!

But by the sixteenth century a change was in the atmosphere and it came from Italy. Certainly we can hear the desire to write with stronger feeling in the music of di Rore and Gesualdo.

But the Italians were also beginning to break down the regimentation of tempi, at least this seems clear in Praetorius' *Syntagma Musicum* (1619), which he wrote as a kind of introductory treatise for the purpose of introducing the Italian style to Germany. When discussing various signatures at the beginning of compositions, Praetorius finds there is no longer agreement among the Italians. He suggests that the slower common time signature is used in madrigals and the faster alla-breve sign is used in motets.[27] However, he has noticed that in all the compositions of Gabrieli, he uses only the alla-breve sign. In the works of Viadana, he finds the alla-breve sign in compositions with text and the common time sign in instrumental works. His own opinion, agreeing with what he has found in the works of Lassus and Marenzio, was that,

[27] Ibid., 48ff.

> the common time sign should be used for those motets and
> other sacred compositions which have many black notes,
> in order to show that the beat is to be taken more slowly ...
> Anyone, however, may reflect upon such matters himself and
> decide, on the basis of text and music, where the beat has to be
> slow and where fast.

His last sentence is revolutionary, for we can see that the question of tempo has now passed from the composer to the performer.

In concerti, where madrigal and motets styles are found, it is necessary to change tempo. Here, instead of using the common

time and alla-breve signs, Praetorius suggests it might be better to employ the new practice of using Italian words, such as adagio, presto, etc.[28]

Praetorius clearly reflects[29] a level of *rubato* never mentioned in earlier treatises. For this practice he makes two general rules: first, that a performance must not be hurried, and second, that all note values must be observed. Then he adds a comment that demonstrates how dramatic the revolution in the approach to tempo was. The conductor can now decide for himself changes in tempo with are entirely un-notated in the score.

> But to use, by turns, now a slower, now a faster beat, in accordance with the text, lends dignity and grace to a performance and makes it admirable ... Some do not want such mixture of [tempi] in any one composition. But I cannot accept their opinion, especially since it makes motets and concerti particularly delightful, when after some slow and expressive measures at the beginning several quick phrases follow, succeeded in turn by slow and stately ones, which again change off with faster ones.

This apparent new freedom among the Italians is confirmed by the many similar Baroque recommendations to the performer to feel free to vary the tempo. The whole story of the Baroque Period, music history texts notwithstanding, was a fervent attempt to return emotions to music, after fifteen centuries of their being discouraged by the Church. And so the very nature of these recommendations reflect a prior regimentation in the concept of tempo, which the Baroque composers seemed eager to destroy. The very practice Praetorius discusses above, relative to the freedom of the performer to make his own decision on tempo, had been mentioned four years earlier, in 1615, by Frescobaldi:

> These pieces should not be played to a strict beat any more than modern madrigals which, though difficult, are made easier by taking the beat now slower, now faster, and by even pausing altogether in accordance with the expression and meaning of the text.[30]

We wish to emphasize that the reason for this new freedom in tempo was to aid in the expression of emotion. One feels this clearly in Monteverdi, as well as his concern about the old style of rigid tempi, when he pleads that his song must be "sung to the time of the heart's feeling, and not to that of the hand."[31] And we find exactly the same plea by Giovanni Bonachelli in 1642:

> In accordance with the feeling one must guide the beat, sensing it now fast, now slow, according to the occasion, now liveliness, and now languor, as indeed anyone will easily know immediately who possesses the fine manner of singing.[32]

By 1676, the great English critic, Thomas Mace, seems to suggest that this new freedom now also included decisions on the tempo of larger formal sections of the music. If, he says, the music falls into sections, these may be played,

> According as they best please your own fancy, some very briskly, and courageously, and some again gently, lovingly, tenderly and smoothly.

He then continues with the same recommendation to the performer we have seen above.

> Beginners must learn strict time; but when we come to be masters, so that we can command all manner of time, at our own pleasures, we then take liberty to break time; sometimes faster and sometimes slower, as we perceive the nature of the thing requires.[33]

This new Baroque style of leaving to the performer, not the composer, the decisions regarding tempi in performance is the explanation for what might otherwise seem to the modern reader a rather extraordinary incident involving Haydn in London. Haydn brought new symphonies with him for his second trip to London and when he went to the first rehearsal and, as conductor, sought to give the tempo for a

[31] *Madrigali guerrieri et amorosi*, Venice, 1638.

[32] Giovanni Bonachelli, *Corona di sacri gigli a una, due, tre, Quattro, e cinque voci*, Venice, 1642.

[33] Thomas Mace, *Musick's Monument* [1676] (Paris: Editions du Centre National de la Recherche Scientifique, 1966), 429, 432.

manuscript work never before seen by the orchestra, he was immediately overruled by the "Leader" (the Koncertmeister) who considered it his job to set the tempo. There must have developed some conflict for it carried over into a debate in the local newspapers. One who defended Haydn's right to set the tempo of his own music was the famous Charles Burney:

> There is a censure leveled at him … for marking the measure to his own new composition: but as even the old compositions had never been performed under his direction, in this country, till the last winter, it was surely allowable for him to indicate to the orchestra the exact time in which he intended the several movements to be played, without offending the leader or subalterns of the excellent band which he had to conduct.

During the nineteenth century we again find famous composers arguing for freedom in tempo, as we see, for example, in a letter by von Weber to the music director, Praeger, in Leipzig.

> The beat must not be like a tyrannical hammer, impeding or urging on, but must be to the music what the pulse-beat is to the life of man. There is no slow tempo in which passages do not occur that demand a quicker motion, so as to obviate the impression of dragging. Conversely there is no presto that does not need a quiet delivery by many places, so as not to throw away the chance of expressiveness by hurrying … Neither the quickening nor the slowing of the tempo should ever give the impression of the spasmodic or the violent. The changes, to have a musical-poetic significance, must come in an orderly way in periods and phrases, conditioned by the varying warmth of the expression.[34]

[34] Quoted in Felix Weingartner, *On Conducting* (New York: Kalmus), 41.

Richard Wagner complained that the "conductor-guild" of his time dictated that there should be no tempo modification in the music of Beethoven, a view he attributed to the "incapacity and general unfitness of our conductors themselves."[35] This attitude is still very strong in Europe, where it is presently heard in the advice that with regard to the master composers one should play only "what they wrote."

[35] William Ashton Ellis, *Wagner's Prose Works,* (New York: Broude), IV, 336. The present writer, as a young conductor, once received a brutal tongue-lashing from Eugene Ormandy for creating a slight, brief cadential *ritard.* while conducting the Philadelphia Orchestra in the first movement of Beethoven's Fourth Symphony.

Finally, after Brahms conducted his own Fourth Symphony with the famous Meiningen Orchestra he wrote Joseph Joachim complaining, of things not notated in the score, "In these concerts I couldn't make enough slowings and accelerations."[36] And anyone who has heard the extant recording of Mahler playing at the piano a transcription of his own Fifth Symphony will have been astonished to hear tempi, and tempo alteration so radical as to be virtually unrecognizable in the score.

[36] *Johannes Brahms im Briefwechsel mit Joseph Joachim* (Berlin, 1908), II, 205.

After reading all these similar comments by really great musicians, we hope the reader who is a musician will pause to contemplate on the degree which the twentieth century has taken something away from him and given it back to the composer. Or have we performers just lost sight of something?

The most serious consequence of the Church's decision to make music a branch of mathematics, as a part of its campaign against the emotions, was the creation of the modern notational system by church mathematicians. Adhering to the Church dogma, they created a notational system without a single symbol which has anything to do with emotion or feeling. Having to notate music with such an incomplete system forced composers to seek other, less effective, means of communicating with performers, such as the language at the beginning of the score. Couperin makes these same points in the preface to his *L'Art de Toucher.*

> Not having devised signs or characters for communicating our specific ideas, we try to remedy this by indicating at the beginning of our pieces, by some such word as Tenderly, Quickly, etc., as far as possible the idea we want to convey.

The most familiar form of this practice to musicians is, of course, what Praetorius calls in 1619, "the new practice of using Italian words, such as adagio, presto, etc." For musicians today these Italian words convey tempo, but originally they were intended to reflect character, not speed.[37] It will be quite surprising for the reader to see how Johann Mattheson (1681–1764) defined some of these familiar terms,

[37] Only a few, such as "grave," today carry a character association.

An Adagio indicates distress; a Lamento lamentation; a Lento
relief; an Andante hope; an Affetuoso love; an Allegro comfort; a
Presto eagerness.[38]

[38] Johann Mattheson, *Der vollkommene Capellmeister* (1739), trans. Ernest Harriss (Ann Arbor: UMI Research Press, 1981), II, xii, 34ff.

Whatever the original intent of these words were, their meaning had already become lost, according to Leopold Mozart, by
1756.[39]

[39] See his violin treatise.

Things were made a bit more confusing during the Baroque
by the French vocabulary used in place of the Italian terms.
In particular, the word, "Movement," by which, according to
Mattheson, the French meant "what the Italians commonly
indicate only with some adjectives such as: affettuoso, con
discrezione, con spirito."[40]

[40] Johann Mattheson, op. cit., II, vii, 7.

In other words, Movement meant the emotional quality and
did not refer to speed or tempo. It is in this sense that when we
speak of the "First Movement," or "Second Movement," in a
Mozart symphony, for example, we are reflecting the original
intent which was "first emotion" and "second emotion."
There may have been more correspondence of such terms with
tempo than we might think today. We have known Europeans
who say "First tempo" and "Second tempo" when referring
to the two principal sections of the sonata form in Classical
symphonies.

With this in mind we can understand the title of a book quoted
by Mattheson, *Les mouvements differents sont le pur espirit de la
Musique.*[41] Mattheson himself says movement is a "spiritual
thing," not a physical thing, and depends not on "precepts
and prohibitions," but "feeling and emotion." To find the
correct movement, the performer must "probe and feel his
own soul" as well as "feel the various impulses which the
piece is supposed to express."[42] The ability to correctly find
the movement, Mattheson observes, is a knowledge which
"transcends all words" and "is the highest perfection of music,
and it can be attained only through considerable experience
and great gifts."

[41] Jean Rousseau, *Methode claire, certaine et facile pour apprendre a chanter la musique* (Paris, 1678).

[42] *Der vollkommene Capellmeister*, op. cit., II, vii, 18ff.

By refusing to use the Italian terms, the French apparently created some confusion among their own ranks. Couperin, for instance, explains,

> I find we confuse Measure or Time with what is called Cadence or Movement. Measure defines the number and quality of the beats; and Cadence is literally the intelligence and the soul which must be added to it.[43]

We find this same concern expressed in Jean Rousseau's viole treatise of 1687.

> There are people who imagine that imparting the movement is to follow and keep time; but these are very different matters, for it is possible to keep time without entering into the movement, since time depends on the music, but the movement depends on genius and fine taste.

Sebastien de Brossard, in an early dictionary of music (1703), considered time from a different perspective with regard to the recitative. Writing of rubato in Largo tempo, he observes,

> In Italian recitatives we often do not make the beats very equal, because this is a kind of declamation where the Actor ought to follow the movement of the passion which inspires him or which he wants to express, rather than that of an equal and regulated measure.[44]

With the hope to bring order to the general confusion regarding the designation of tempi there were a number of private inventors, caught up in the enthusiasm of the Industrial Revolution at the beginning of the nineteenth century, who worked toward creating a mechanical device for standardizing tempo. The winner of this race was the quack-inventor, acquaintance of Beethoven and emigrant to America, Johann Maelzel.[45] Maelzel's metronome held promise for some, but for authentic musicians it only represented another rigid form of tyranny contradictory to musical feeling. Beethoven, for example, who

[43] François Couperin, *L'Art de toucher* (Paris, 1717, reprinted Wiesbaden: Breitkopf & Härtel, 1933), 24.

[44] Sebastien de Brossard, *Dictionaire de Musique* (Paris, 1703), "Largo."

[45] He more or less stole the idea from Dietrich Winkel of Amsterdam.

made the instrument known, wrote on a score following the indication, "100 according to Maelzel,"

> But this must be held applicable to only the first measures, for feeling also has its tempo and this cannot entirely be expressed in this figure.[46]

[46] Quoted in Erich Leinsdorf, *The Composer's Advocate* (New Haven: Yale University Press, 1981, 165.

Beethoven may have revised his thinking with more experience, for Franz Liszt claimed that when asked about the metronome, Beethoven replied, "Better none."[47]

[47] Letter to Breitkopf & Härtel, Nov. 16, 1863.

Here is a sampling of later views:

Berlioz,

> I do not mean to say that it is necessary to imitate the mathematical regularity of the metronome, which would give the music thus executed an icy frigidity; I even doubt whether it would be possible to maintain this rigid uniformity for more than a few bars.[48]

[48] His *Essay on Conducting.*

Brahms, regarding his *Requiem*,

> I think ... that the metronome is of no value ... The so-called "elastic" tempo is moreover not a new invention.[49]

[49] Ibid., 129.

Verdi, a note in his *Te Deum*,

> This entire piece ought to be performed in one tempo as indicated by the metronome. This notwithstanding, it will be appropriate to broaden or accelerate in certain spots for reasons of expression and nuance.[50]

[50] Ibid., 130.

Wagner, regarding his *Tannhäuser*,

> As to the "tempi" of the whole work in general, I can only say that if conductor and singers are to depend for their time on the metronomical marks alone, the spirit of the work must stand indeed in sorry case.[51]

[51] *Prose Works of Wagner*, III, 190.

Bruno Walter,

The metronome marking is good only for the first few bars.[52]

[52] *On Music and Music-Making* (New York: Norton, 1957), 43.

Erich Leinsdorf,

I do not consult the little clock.[53]

[53] Leinsdorf, op. cit., 130.

Well, the metronome is a horrible concept, a return to rigid formalism and the tyranny of rules. It is also unnecessary, for all the information on tempo is already provided by the composer—in the music itself. Thus, Franz Liszt wrote to a correspondent,

> A metronomical performance is certainly tiresome and nonsensical; time and rhythm must be adapted to and identified with the melody, the harmony, the accent and the poetry.[54]

[54] Letter to Siegmund Lebert, Jan. 10, 1870.

And, when one considers the general limitation of our notational system, perhaps Mendelssohn said it best when he admits ignoring the notation completely,

> I think the movement might be taken too slow, which I found to be the case at the first rehearsal, until I no longer paid any attention to the notes or the heading, but adhered to the sense alone.[55]

[55] Letter to Nicolas Gade, March 3, 1843.

So where does this leave us today? Are we allowed to make alterations in tempo within a movement? Yes we are, for as Beethoven said, "feeling has its own tempo." One arrives at the tempo from the music itself and from nothing else. But we caution, this is an aspect of musicianship and you will be so judged by the listener.

For discovering tempo while studying scores I recommend, in places of doubt, singing. Singing somehow brings us into touch with the universal aspects of music and one should put some faith in your own inner, genetic, feeling in this regard. Certainly any form of classroom theoretical analysis will reveal nothing of tempo.

The Symbols *f* and **p**: What do they Signify?

MUSIC STUDENTS IN THE UNITED STATES are introduced to the symbols of dynamics, **p**, *f*, **mp**, **mf**, etc., as if they were part of a scientific measure of volume of sound, **p** being soft and *f* being loud. I recall in my youth often during the rehearsal of a strain in a march hearing the conductor say, "loud the first time through and soft the second time through," as if that were the end of interpretation of the music. But if we keep in mind that the purpose of music is to communicate feelings and emotions, then clearly to speak of relative decibels of the volume of sound is to speak in a different language. And in any case it is important to remember that any real precision in the measurement of dynamic symbols is impossible because they are all relative, as Debussy made clear in the "Serenade for the Doll" of his *Children's Corner,* when he specified,

> Use the soft pedal throughout the whole piece, even at the places marked forte.

Since *piano* and *forte* are Italian words, perhaps we should begin asking what these words mean in the lives of ordinary Italian citizens. Beginning with the definition for *piano*, my *Cassell's Italian-English Dictionary* gives several, unnumbered, non-preferential one-word definitions, beginning, as we might expect, with softly. The second one-word definition, gently, is a surprise for this has a distinctly subjective character and is closer to the meaning found in conversation of Italians today. If one were to say, in an attempt to quiet down a group of people, "piano, piano," the speaker would be understood to mean something more like "calm down," and not "softer, softer."

The third one-word definition is even more of a surprise— slowly! Have you ever had a teacher point to the lowercase *p* in a composition and tell you it means slow? On the other hand, the thousands of Classical Period symphonies, concerti and chamber works one knows, one recalls that the second movement, which is almost invariably slow, begins with a lowercase *p* at the beginning. Certainly no one of us has ever said to a class, "We are now going to hear the soft movement of Mozart's Symphony No. 40."

Similarly, my dictionary gives for *forte* a number of one-word definitions: strong (which my wife, Giselle, reminds me is the same in Spanish: *un hombre fuerte* is a strong man), followed by vigorous, powerful, sturdy, robust, hale, healthy, considerable, large, heavy, high and even angry. But notice how all of them are subjective and it is striking that only the twelfth of these one-word definitions reads, "loud (of sound)."

In earlier music one finds it is frequently these subjective words which are associated with dynamics. The second-century poem by Longus, *Daphnis and Chloe,* has a panpipe player, in contrast to his powerful, loud sound, is now playing at a sweet, soft level. Similarly, Chaucer, in his fourteenth century, *Canterbury Tales,* has Absalom singing in a small and gentle voice.

Monteverdi, in 1638, found the "principal passions or emotions of the soul to be three, namely, anger, serenity and humility." These, he says, "the art of music clearly manifests in three terms: agitated, soft and moderate." Please notice that Monteverdi wrote agitated, and not *forte*.

Georg Muffat, in the Foreword to his collection of concerti, *Auserlesene Instrumental-Music* (1701) suggests remarkable extremes of soft and loud, but nevertheless he still emphasizes the subjective qualities of tenderness and vehemence.

> At the direction *piano* or *p* all are ordinarily to play at once so softly and tenderly that one barely hears them, and at the direction *forte* or *f* with so full a tone, from the first note so marked, that the listeners are left, as it were, astounded at such vehemence.

It was also the case that in earlier times the selection of the dynamics was considered to be a matter to be decided by the performer, not the composer. This same freedom in performance allowed in tempo is also extended to dynamics, according to Praetorius.

> Besides, it adds much charm to harmony and melody, if the dynamic level in the vocal and instrumental parts is varied now and then.

Praetorius returns to the subject of dynamics, in another place, mentioning that the Italians are beginning to use *forte*, *piano*, etc., to mark changes within a concerto. It is interesting that, once again, he suggests that the conductor is free to alter both dynamics and tempo.

> I rather like this practice. There are some who believe that this is not very appropriate, especially in churches. I feel, however, that such variety [in dynamics] and change [in tempo] are not only agreeable and proper, if applied with moderation and designed to express the feelings of the music, and affect the ear and the spirit of the listener much more and give the concerto a unique quality and grace. Often the composition itself, as well as the text and the meaning of the words, requires that one [change] at times—but not too frequently or excessively—beating now fast, now slowly, also that one lets the choir by turns sing quietly and softly, and loudly and briskly. To be sure, in churches there will be more need of restraint in such changes than at banquets.[56]

[56] Ibid., 132 (112).

It is also interesting here, that Praetorius gives one Latin term, *lento gradu*, which he understood to mean that the voice was both softer and slower.

What is important to observe here is that the earlier musicians had a much broader perspective of the dynamic symbols than we do with our tendency to just say "loud" and "soft." Further, their broader perspective resulted in some important characteristics of performance which we seem to have lost today. First, the individual dynamic symbol was used with a much broader range of meaning than we use today. For example the *forte* symbol, according to K. P. E. Bach, was also used as a symbol of accent, being used under unusual dissonances, to accent some "violent turn of the melody," to emphasize deceptive cadences, and under non-harmonic tones.[57]

[57] K. P. E. Bach, *The Art of Keyboard Playing*, trans. William J. Mitchell, (New York: Norton, 1949), 163.

The second way in which this earlier more subjective perspective of the traditional dynamic symbols resulted in performance practice which was quite different from today is that while we take these symbols as a kind of road sign—something happens here—the earlier musicians simply incorporated them into their broader interpretation of the musical passage at hand. Thus, what a contemporary of J. S. Bach, heard, you will not see on paper:

> All who have heard Bach play the Clavichord must have been struck by the endless nuances of shadow and light that he casts over his performance.[58]

[58] Johann F. Cramer, *Magazin der Musik*, I, p. 1217.

A contemporary of Bach's son, K. P. E. Bach, Johann Joachim Quantz used the same images:

> Light and shadow must be constantly be maintained ... a continual alternation of the Forte and Piano must be observed ... In the majority of pieces one Passion constantly alternates with another, the performer must know how to judge the nature of the Passion that each thought [*pensée* in the French edition; *Gedanken* in the German edition] contains, and constantly make his execution conform to it.[59]

[59] Johann Joachim Quantz, *Essay on how to Learn to Play the Traversière Flûte* [1752], II, 14 and 15.

An early account by Roger North (1585–1652) suggests this practice was in place a generation before Bach.

> Learn to fill, and soften a sound, as shades in needlework, in sensation, so as to be like also a gust of wind, which begins with soft air, and fills by degrees to a strength as makes all bend, and then softens away again into a temperate level.[60]

[60] Roger North, *Autobiography* [c. 1695], Jessopp, London, 1887, sect. 106.

And a contemporary of Bach, makes the point that these "shades" are needed emotionally.

> Yet it is to be observed that with both [forte and piano] one should not fall suddenly from piano into forte but gradually strengthen the voice, and then again let it drop so the consequently, on those notes where such [effects] are needed the piano comes before the forte which comes in the middle and the passage must again be ended with piano.[61]

[61] Wolfgang Michael Mylius, *Rudiments Musices*, Gotha, 1686, p. 49.

Further, the Baroque player appears to have felt the freedom to add or change dynamic markings to fit his interpretation.

> We play Loud or Soft, according to our fancy, or the mood of the music.[62]
>
> .....
>
> Humour a Lesson [composition] by Playing some Sentences Loud and others again Soft, according as they best please your own fancy.[63]

[62] Christopher Simpson, *Divison-Violist*, London, 1659, 10.

[63] Thomas Mace, *Musick's Monument*, London, 1676, 130.

Quantz in his famous flute treatise reminds the reader that in most cases there are no dynamic markings in the original and that it is important that the performer "work out a good scheme of louds and softs." But he then continues with a very interesting observation,

> But within these fairly level planes of volume, a constant play of light and shade can keep the dynamic texture alive with interest.[64]

[64] Quantz, op. cit., VII, 23.

And so, as we began above, the listener would be "struck by the endless nuances of shadow and light" that Bach casts over his performance.

This presents us with an interesting and important question: How did we lose sight of something so fundamental? How did we evolve away from making dynamic levels part of the "needlework" of interpretation?[65]

One answer may lie with the organ, which became popular in the Baroque Period. The early organ did not have the *crescendo* pedal of the modern instrument. One could set the stops to produce a *piano* dynamic level which could then not be altered by the fingers while playing. Bach could not have done on the organ what he did on the Clavichord. If an organist wanted a *forte*, by hitting a lever suddenly a dozen or more small windows above the organist, portals to the pipe chamber, would fly open and the listeners would be struck with an immediate blast of much louder sound. Thus, Joachim Quantz recalled in 1752 that it was still common practice for organists to perform "terrace dynamics," long stretches at a single level before changing to a long stretch at another level.

Certainly an important factor in the loss of our freedom of interpretation has been the introduction in the nineteenth century of the futile and anti-musical concept of holding "contests" in music. This has resulted, in the United States, in an ethic by which an ensemble is graded not on the basis of musicality, but on the basis of performing exactly and precisely what appears on paper. *Forte* must be loud, *piano* must be on the border of inaudibility or a demerit is given. No one seems to care if there were any musical purpose to these symbols. Here I must mention an occasion when I was engaged to be the President of the Jury for an international piano contest in Italy. The other ten judges were all famous piano teachers; I was to represent the "general listener." After a moving and musical performance of a Beethoven Sonata by a pianist from Finland [who, upon a vote of 10 to 1, was thrown out and sent home] I turned to one of the judges whom I knew, a performing artist

[65] We pass over the modern music education theories which have eliminated the role of communication of feelings in performance in the classroom to be replaced by "conceptual music education theory," which means primarily teaching only descriptions of the grammar of music and not the performance of music.

from Argentina, and asked him how the entire jury, excepting myself, rejected so musical a performance. "Oh," he answered in a most matter of fact voice, "piano contests have nothing to do with music!"

Finally, I would like to share an example consisting of the final four bars of the first movement of an original Baroque band composition by Johann Müller.

Figure 23: Johann Michael Müller, *Concerto da Camera XII*

If you were trained as a conductor as I was, to prepare each change one preparation gesture before the event, you would look at this music, and after contemplating the rehearsal time involved to achieve this, not to mention the conducting acrobatics, and you would think to yourself, "No, I will not perform this composition."

But if one were to view this music from the perspective of earlier performance practice one would not see these *pianos* and *fortes* as road signs, but rather only as variations of emotional intensity. And in the case, because the tempo is Allegro these variations might be relative small in size—repeated chord tones which lean forward slightly with more emotional intensity and then pull back with less emotional intensity—a gentle forward back, forward back, etc., concluding with perhaps a *ritardando* on the final two beats. The result would be a lovely and elegant coda to this movement.

Today it is still true that there is enormous liberty in performance when it comes to dynamics because all the symbols are relative and without any precise definitions. Everyone has his own definition of *piano* and *forte*.

Today, with this freedom of choice among symbols which have no agreed upon definition, how does one make decisions about dynamics in one's own performance or in one's teaching? In one famous attempt to create method in this, Marcel Tabeteau, former Principal Oboe of the Philadelphia Orchestra, used to give his students a melody and then require them to number each note, 1 through 10, with ten being the most important melodic note in their view. This is very difficult, requiring one to constantly change one's mind about some insignificant looking note on the way to the climax, "no, this is a 3, not a 4," etc.

Conscious or unconscious, one has to do this with every phrase one plays or conducts. The difficulty is that we are not trained to think like this in our youth. We are trained to see a symbol on paper and obey it. The symbol's emotional meaning if not discussed, which can result in years of practicing and playing, devoid of music.

We must learn to think of these symbols as expressions of the heart, not of science.

How to Bring to Life Dead Notation

IN THE FIELD OF MUSIC, agogic accentuation refers to the emphasis of important melodic notes. We often forget this due to the concentration on an instrument we are holding or on the demands for accuracy in performance, etc., but we all know what this principle is from our experience with normal speech. Take a sentence like, "I am going to go buy a hamburger." If you repeat this each time emphasizing a different word the meaning of the sentence is dramatically changed. "I am going to go *buy* a hamburger" (as opposed to getting a free one). "I am going to go buy *a* hamburger" (as opposed to buying two or more), etc. The same idea using pauses creates new meanings, as in the following example. "What is this thing called love?" "What, is this thing called love?" "What is this thing called, love?"

This agogic principle of emphasis may be very old. It is easy to imagine early man, before language when he was making only vowel-like utterances, making some small distinctions through his right brain choice of emphasis on a single vowel sound, such as "oh," "Oh!," "oh?" or "Ooooo." Later, when man had developed a spoken language, but still before the development of written languages, he surely continued in this same right hemisphere emphasis as a control of meaning, for we still do this today—we carry this from early man.

This principle must have been crucial in ancient literature, such as with Homer, that immortal blind Greek poet, the author of the *Iliad* and the *Odyssey*. These epic stories were created before the advent of the written Greek language and were so passed down in an oral tradition for some two centuries until there was an available way to write them down. They were passed down by an extraordinary kind of performer called a Rhapsodist, one who is called a musician, never an orator and never a singer in the modern sense. The Rhapsodist delivered these epics from memory before audiences and, according to Plato's book *Ion,* named for a Rhapsodist, in which Socrates has a discussion with an actual Rhapsodist, they were creating strong emotional reactions in their listeners.

SOCRATES: I wish you would frankly tell me, Ion, what I am going to ask you: When you produce the greatest effect upon the audience in the recitation of some striking passage, such as the apparition of Odysseus leaping forth on the floor, recognized by the suitors and shaking out his arrows at his feet, or the description of Achilles springing upon Hector, or the sorrows of Andromache, Hecuba, or Priam,—are you in your right mind? Are you not carried out of yourself, and does not your soul in an ecstasy seem to be among the persons or places of which you are speaking ...?

IoN: That proof strikes home to me, Socrates. For I must frankly confess that at the tale of pity my eyes are filled with tears, and when I speak of horrors, my hair stands on end and my heart throbs.

SOCRATES: Well, Ion, and what are we to say of a man who at a sacrifice or festival, when he is dressed in an embroidered robe, and has golden crowns upon his head, of which nobody has robbed him, appears weeping and panic-stricken in the presence of more than twenty thousand friendly faces, when there is no one despoiling or wronging him;—is he in his right mind or is he not?

IoN: No indeed, Socrates, I must say that, strictly speaking, he is not in his right mind.

SOCRATES: And are you aware that you produce similar effects on most of the spectators?

Ion: Only too well; for I look down upon them from the stage, and behold the various emotions of pity, wonder, sternness, stamped upon their faces when I am performing: and I am obliged to give my very best attention to them; for if I make them cry I myself shall laugh, and if I make them laugh I myself shall cry, when the time of payment arrives.[66]

[66] *Ion,* 534, c - 535e.

We can no longer know exactly what the Rhapsodists were doing in terms of their vocal technique, but I am always reminded of the Rhapsodist when I look at our oldest European music notation, those ninth-century neumes, which no one today knows how to transcribe. Those characters do not look like meter or beats to me, so much as symbols to indicate performance, the pitch of individual syllables.[67] And if they are a system of symbols to indicate, not what to sing, but how to sing certain syllables then the information which came down from that remarkable early scholar, Roger Bacon (1220–1292) may be a clue to confirm that explanation for the neumes. He made the very interesting observation,

[67] Whenever I hear ancient Chinese opera, with its extremely wide tessitura and great variety of vocal sounds, I wonder if it is the last remnant of the old vocal production of the Rhapsodist.

For accent is a kind of singing; whence it is called accent from accino, accinis [I sing, thou singest], because every syllable has its own proper sound either raised, lowered, or composite, and all syllables of one word are adapted or sung to one syllable on which rests the principal sound.[68]

[68] *The Opus Majus of Roger Bacon,* trans. Robert Burke (New York: Russell & Russell, 1962), I, 259.

If there was a system such as Bacon implies, where "every syllable has its own sound," then one can imagine perhaps the text of *The Odyssey* composing the music itself.

There are a few more references we should consider. The sixth-century AD Greek writer, Paulus Silentiarius, wrote a poem in honor of a deceased lyre player, which mentions an interesting reference to music being the origin of grammar, recognizing that feelings in speech came before rules of grammar.

Damocharis passed into the final silence of Fate; alas! The Muses' love lyre is silent: the holy foundation of Grammar has perished.

Guido of Arezzo, in his eleventh-century *Micrologus,* the first modern notation system to follow the neume system, mentions another vocal characteristic we carry from ancient man, the fact that we often have an unconscious raising of the pitch of the voice in states of fear or excitement. Guido adds a curious and very interesting psychological observation.

> We often place an acute or grave accent above the notes, because we often utter them with more or less stress, so much so that the repetition of the same note often seems to be a raising or lowering.[69]

By the way, it is in this treatise that we find the earliest reference to a *ritard.* at the end of a composition.

> Towards the ends of phrases the notes should always be more widely spaced as they approach the breathing place, like a galloping horse, so that they arrive at the pause, as it were, weary and heavily.[70]

In the *Compendium Musices,* of 1552, by Adrian Coclico, a treatise written to train boys to sing in Church, we again find a reference to placing specific music under a specific syllable.

> When he has learned these things clearly and rapidly, he will then begin to sing, not only as [the music] is written but also with embellishments, and to pronounce skillfully, smoothly and meaningfully, to intone correctly and to place any syllable in its proper place under the right notes.[71]

The final two early references to this connection known to me come from the sixteenth century. Tinctoris (1435–1511) makes an incredible definition, "A melodic interval is the immediate connection of one syllable after another."[72]

And, finally, Erasmus (1466–1536) writes,

> The accent can justifiably be called, as it was by some ancient grammarians, the soul of the word.[73]

[69] *Hucbald, Guido and John on Music,* trans. Warren Babb (New Haven: Yale University Press, 1978) 139.

[70] Ibid., 175.

[71] Adrian Coclico, *Musical Compendium,* trans. Albert Seay (Colorado Spring: Colorado College Music Press, 1973), 6.

[72] Tinctoris, *Dictionary of Musical Terms,* trans. Carl Parrish (New York: Free Press of Glencoe, 1963), 17.

[73] "The Right Way of Speaking Latin and Greek," [1528] in ibid., XXVI, 422ff.

Because the above discussion spans more than two thousand years we cannot know for certain what the earliest practice was with regard to using pitch, or music, to clarify meaning. What we are left with today is the agogic accent principle which, if not genetic, is in any case a very natural tool in performance to express meaning. But only if one uses it. As we have noted above, Music is not a thing, it is an act, it is something we do. How we place an agogic accent, or emphatic lingering, within a melody distinguishes our own individual interpretations of the music on paper. But what if you elect to perform and add nothing in the way of agogic accents? Bruce Haynes compares the written form of the music to a cookbook and therefore observes that if one does nothing in shaping the melody, then instead of making a cake, one is eating the cookbook.

Can one go too far? The Modernists of the twentieth century thought so and, believe it or not, the Vienna Conservatory in the early 1960s formed a *Stilkommission* which had among its goals the elimination of the "agogic freedom of the Liszt-school." With the Modernists School, of course, the pendulum swung too far in the opposite direction giving us a century of pretty dull music making.

Finally, I should like to mention that there are some accentuations which are inherent in the notation itself. The reader can easily find many treatises on ornaments, for example, Johann Mattheson in the seventeenth century already complained,

> In the past our learned musicians have compiled whole books ... on nothing but vocal ornaments.[74]

74 Johann Mattheson, *Der vollkommene Capellemeister* [1739], II, 14, 50-51.

I will not repeat the most familiar of these practices, but do want to make two observations. First, I often have had students tell me that their private teachers have told them that all eighteenth-century trills are upper-note trills. That is not correct. Baroque trills are very clearly upper-note trills, but Classical Period trills are without question main-note trills in principle.

I also want to mention the portamento, which is not familiar to wind conductors. The portamento is an unbroken slide from beneath to the note to be accented and which was used extensively in the nineteenth century by singers and string players.[75] Beginning in the 1930s it was identified as a characteristic of the Romantic style and thus retired by the Modernists. For wind conductors I should like to point out the use of written out portamento in the fourth movement of the *Suite Française* by Darius Milhaud. The written out portamento in the bass instruments in m. 43, and in similar places, reflecting a chill going up the spine, should be on the fast side, with no noticeable changes in pitch, that is, a smooth slide (Fig. 23).

[75] I have a recording of the last castrato made about 1904 which employs this frequently. I also have a recording from the 1920s of Ormandy, as a violinist, adding the portamento to increase emotion. He continued to use this principle frequently as a conductor.

Figure 24: Darius Milhaud, *Suite Française*, mm. 42–45

The other portamento is the melodic one in m. 44 (Fig. 24), and especially after m. 97 (Fig. 25). This one is purely melodic, and is a painful cry. It should be performed very slowly, without pitch distinction and with a *crescendo*.

Figure 25: Darius Milhaud, *Suite Française,* mm. 43–45

Figure 26: Darius Milhaud, *Suite Française,* mm. 96–99

Written Accents

Before any kind of articulation was added to notes on paper, the wind instrument players were practicing articulation through the pronunciation of syllables, known as syllabication, which may be yet another remnant of the above discussion on the treatment of syllables through pitch. It was essential in the performance of the early cornetto, which was played from the side of the mouth and thus inaccessible to the tongue. The famous sixteenth-century book on cornetto improvisation by Dalla Casa includes pages of music with syllables underneath for the player to practice before getting to the actual repertoire of the book. A modern example is that of a nineteenth-century English flute teacher who taught the student to say the word "territory" while playing four eighth-notes slurred two by two on paper. The sound of "territory," in my twenty-first century English, suggests that the result was that the first eighth-note was slightly louder and longer than the remaining notes, with the third eighth-note being slightly louder than numbers two and four.

This last example reminds us of the thirteenth bar of the oboe in the Adagio in the Mozart "Gran Partita," K. 361. First I should remind the reader that this figure is really the only true consistent appoggiatura used by Mozart, everything else is generally intended to be grace notes. As I suppose all musicians know, the appoggiatura slurred to an eighth-note and two sixteenth-notes was intended always to be performed as four sixteenth-notes, with the first two slurred, with the first note accented.

Figure 27: Mozart, "Gran Partita", m. 13, Oboe 1, manuscript.

Mozart wrote it this way, and not as four sixteenth-notes, as that was one of the few recognized ways to indicate an accent. Four sixteenths written would be played two slurred and two tongued, but without an accent.

Figure 28: Mozart, "Gran Partita", m. 13, Oboe 1, with applied performance practice.

A noticeable proof of this can be seen in m. 17 of the Adagio where he writes four sixteenth-notes. When this material returns in the recapitulation one can see that Mozart first wrote in the oboe a G appoggiatura above the staff. Then he remembered he did not want an accent on this figure, so he crosses out the G appoggiatura and replaces it with a regular G, now part of four written out sixteenth notes.

Figure 29: Mozart, "Gran Partita", m. 40, Oboe 1.

To return to m. 13 and the similarity with "territory," one can see in the principal oboe two appoggiaturas, one written as an eighth-note with one slash through it and the next one with two slashes through it. Mozart was not always entirely consistent in the matter of the number of slashes, as one can see in the basset horn in mm. 14 and 23. Again, returning to the oboe in m. 1s, the result of course will be two slurred sixteenth-notes, with the first one accented and two tongued ones, followed by two slurred ones and two tongued ones. But we can't help wondering if in writing first an eighth-note with one slash, rather than two slashes as in the following figure, he meant that the first of the eight sixteenth-notes is longer than the fifth one (with two slashes). Perhaps this is "territory" on some earlier German word.

Mozart is also not entirely consistent in the use of the remaining familiar accent symbols, the *fp* and *sfp*.[76] Generally these kinds of mistakes in Mozart I attribute to the speed in writing this secondary data while his head is racing ahead with new melodic material. He was surely bored with this level of calligraphy, as one can see in the beginning of the "Gran Partita" when he went back later to fill in the horn parts. Here, with stems going the wrong way, we recognize speed and not thought.

[76] See the eighteenth bar of the third variation of the Theme and Variations movement, where both *sfp* and *fp* are used in the same bar.

While we do not know the difference Mozart had in mind between *fp* and *sfp*, it is clear that neither one had anything to do with dynamics. The *fp* was an accent at the established dynamic level and not like the modern *fp* which means really a *forte* dynamic level and a *subito piano*. One can see in the fifth bar of the fourth variation of the Theme and Variations movement in the bassoon, Mozart very clearly writes the first eighth-note *forte*, as the climax of the previous *crescendo;* the second eighth-note *piano* to reestablish the *piano* level; and then a *fp* on the third eighth-note, which is clearly an accent at the *piano* level.

In a general sense, the challenge of accentuation is made difficult in cases of inexact notation, or notation which allows a variety of forms in performance. A case in point is the dotted eighth-note connected to a sixteenth-note, which in faster tempi can be played as two sixteenth-notes separated by an eighth-rest and in slow tempi the figure can become almost a triplet with a long second note. Taste is the only rule.

A more difficult example of this same rhythm is found in compound meters where you find connected under one ligature a dotted eighth-note followed by a sixteenth-note followed a a regular eighth-note. This is a very difficult rhythm to perform accurately, as one can see in its appearance in the Vivace of the first movement of Seventh Symphony of Beethoven where no orchestra plays it correctly; they settle for turning the meter into 4/8.

Performance values versus the written values

Another very important problem in modern performance is an apparent lack of knowledge of the fact that the general style in the eighteenth century consisted of shorter note values than is appropriate in the second half of the nineteenth century. It would be going too far to characterize the basic eighteenth-century style as a modern staccato, but it tended in that direction. Even in keyboard performance if one had four quarter-notes on paper one created a space between the notes.

The ordinary movement consists in lifting the finger from the last key shortly before touching the next note.[77]

[77] F. W. Marpurg, *Anleitung zum Clavier-spielen* (Berlin, 1755, 2nd edition 1765), I, vii, 29.

It is not clear just how "staccato" the Classical Period style of playing was, or where this style originated. Some musicians in Austria told me that they are convinced that the origin was in folk-music and I have heard, high in the mountains, some amateur instrumentalists playing everything really staccato.

There must have been a few musicians during the Classical Period who played the much more legato style we use today, for Quantz mentions it in disapproval calling the notes glued together "like a hurdy gurdy."[78] Certainly today you hear wind players connecting everything, probably thinking the result is more "symphonic," but I call it "Brahmsifying."

[78] Johann Quantz, *The art of flute playing* [1752].

So when did we begin to play earlier music like Brahms? I was told by some distinguished members of the Vienna Philharmonic that this happened shortly after the opera house was first opened in 1869. Apparently the kind of rock used for the interior of the hall, together with the paint, made the winds sound very shrill. After a few years of complaints the hall was repainted and there was some improvement. The winds, nevertheless, found that by lengthening everything the effect was lessened. These same Philharmonic players also taught at the Akademie für Music and so the story goes their students moved across Europe teaching the new style.

The shortening of a note value in the Viennese Classical tradition can be seen in a very important rule: If a note is followed by rests until the next bar line, that note is played half its value. Often this was just shorthand for the scribe. Imagine four eighth-notes, then a bar line, then a quarter-note, with the five notes under a slur. Clearly strings or winds would play this as a group of five eighth-notes under a slur, even though the last note appeared as a quarter-note. But it was quicker for the scribe, and easier to read, if he wrote a quarter-note for otherwise after the bar line he would have to add an additional flag on the note stem and an additional rest.

Figure 30: A written example of a note followed by rests until the next barline.

Figure 31: Figure 29 as played with applied performance practice.

An important example of lengthening a note is found in the double-dotting, a style which continued well through the Classical Period in Vienna. Indeed the performance practice authority, Clive Brown, believes the double-dotting tradition can be traced through the nineteenth century and into the twentieth.[79]

[79] Clive Brown, *Classical and Romantic performing practice.* (Oxford University Press, 1999), 8, 9, 11, 625.

The early music authority, Bruce Haynes, writes at length in protest to those players whose goal is to play exactly what is on paper, which he calls Urtext style.[80]

[80] Haynes, *The End of Early Music.* (Oxford, 2007), 109.

> To play literally "as written" from the page, Urtext style, would thus—paradoxically—be to play not as written, as it would overlook the shorthand messages embedded in the notation and assumed to be understandable.

He is thinking of such things as changing the tempo within a movement, based on feeling and chord changes; note shaping, pauses and two things which he includes under the definition of agogics, which we will discuss below. Here, for Haynes, these include prolonging and making stronger the first of a group of notes in faster passages to clarify the metric groups and delineate figuration, a practice most players do today. He also includes the rhythmic freedom to distinguish melodic ideas. A perfect example can be seen in m. 9 of the Wagner *Trauermusik.* Here one needs to stretch the two sixteenth-notes in order to make them lyrical. To play them as written gives them an instrumental quality. I regard this as a very important practice.

Another place where one needs to feel free to define, usually to lengthen, a note are those places where a note of small value lies just before a whole or half-note in a motive suggesting an announcement, or perhaps the ringing of big bells, the musical representation of "Ta-Ta!" I have a firm conviction that the feeling behind this figure is once again related to movement, to the movement of feet in perhaps a Spanish dance. Try, with both feet together on the floor, lifting the left leg and then in rapid succession returning the left foot to the floor, lifting the right leg and returning the fight foot to the floor. I think, in terms of movement, you will find a natural "feel" for the speed of this dance pattern. The sounds your feet make, in that natural movement, are the sound, I believe, that composers feel in writing this pattern. So, for me whatever length of note the composer wrote before the big principal note, I ignore the appearance on paper and play it the same way, in the speed of that dance step.

Finally, a word on the practice known as inequality, a subject for which the reader can easily find additional information. Basically, this was a very frequently employed Baroque technique to relieve the dull quality of repeated notes on the same pitch. The composer wrote the regular eighth-note version because it was easier than adding an additional note with flag and the triplet symbol. I don't suppose any composer ever thought it would be played as written. I bring up this topic only because in the Baroque Hautboisten band repertoire there are some movements written in imitation of march music, or perhaps in quoting familiar march music. Playing these kinds of passages as written is deadly, but applying inequality allows them to take flight.

"I have a mind to ..."

We all speak well of our hearts, we none of us dare speak well of our minds.[81]
  — La Rochefoucauld (1613–1680)

But though I distrust my head, I am always sure of my heart.[82]
  — Voltaire (1694–1778)

THE PROBLEM UNDERLYING MUCH of human activity is the fact that we have *two* minds, one in the left hemisphere of the brain consisting of a library of rational data, including numbers and words, all learned from other people and all past tense, and the other in the right hemisphere of the brain, a library of personal experiences including those of the present tense. Music is said to be found in both, by which it is meant that music notation, as a rational language, is found in the left hemisphere, while the experience of music is found in the right hemisphere. But is notation really music or is it merely the past tense grammar of music?

Nothing is more fundamental to the performance of music than this subject. Does our performance come from our experience or from the notation? Do we employ feeling or reason when buying a car, buying a house or selecting a spouse?

It is important that the reader not be distracted by continuing brain research studying where various activities are connected to which side of the brain, for with trillions of brain cells this

[81] *The Maxims of La Rochefoucauld,* trans. Louis Kronenberger (New York: Random House, 1959), Nr. 98.

[82] Letter to abbe Chaulieu, July 26, 1717.

kind of research will never end. However, apart from this, the reader must keep in mind that the fact that we have both a bicameral brain, representing both a rational side of ourselves and an experiential side of ourselves will remain recognized as it has been for centuries. Indeed the manifestations are everywhere. The French word for "Law," one of the most conceptual, logical and rational professions, is "droit" ("right" as in right hand[83]), the significance of which is obvious if the reader remembers that the hemispheres of the brain operate opposite sides of the body. Similarly, the Indians of the American Southwest distinguished between the functions of the hands, the right for writing and the left for music. There are the Hindu notions of *buddhi* and *manas* and the Confucian concepts, found in the ancient book, *I Ching,* which associate the masculine, *Yang,* with the left side of the mind and the feminine, *Yin,* with the right. From this comes our expression, "I had a yin to ..." for those actions for which we lack a good rational explanation.

[83] The same association is true in Spanish.

The purpose of the present essay is to bring to the reader's attention just how long this recognition of the rational versus the non-rational sides of man has been part of Western culture.

Among the early Greeks, Epictetus (55–135 AD) was well aware of the rational and non-rational nature of the person and observed, "by nothing is the rational creature so distressed as by the irrational." However, like many early philosophers speculating on how the mind is organized, he arrives at a unique definition. Curiously, a completely rational subject such as grammar he recognizes as something apart from the rational. "Reason" is something he associates more with the id.

Of our faculties in general you will find that none can take cognizance of itself; none therefore has the power to approve or disapprove its own action. Our grammatical faculty for instance: how far can that take cognizance? Only so far as to distinguish expression. Our musical faculty? Only so far as to distinguish tune. Does any one of these then take cognizance of itself? By no means. If you are writing to your friend, when you want to know what words to write grammar will tell you; but whether you should write to your friend or should not write grammar will not tell you. And in the same way music will tell you about tunes, but whether at this precise moment you should sing and play the lyre or should not sing nor play the lyre it will not tell you. What will tell you then?[84]

We are particularly impressed with the insight of Aristides Quintilianus (1st to 4th century AD) who not only recognized the rational and non-rational division,

> These, then, are its two aspects, the rational, through which it accomplishes the works of wisdom, and the irrational, through which it engages in the business of the body.[85]

but he also stated that the "leader and high priest" of the first branch of learning is philosophy and the "ruler" of the second is music.

Cicero, the Roman (106–43 BC), recognizes two divisions in man, but he does not quite know what to call the non-rational side. One can see here the strong prejudice against everything non-rational which has so negatively influenced society.

> The soul is divided into two parts, one of which partakes of reason, the other does not. So when the instruction that we should rule over ourselves is given, the instruction is that reason should restrain impulsiveness. There is in practically everybody's souls by nature something soft, lowly, abject, nerveless so to speak, and feeble. If there were nothing else, a human being would be the ugliest thing that exists. But at hand is the mistress and queen of all, Reason, which through its own strivings advances forward and becomes perfected virtue. It is man's responsibility to ensure that it rules over that part of the soul which ought to obey.[86]

In one of the early music treatises, the *Musica Disciplina* of 843 AD, Aurelian of Reome not only finds that music joins "Reason to the body," but more surprising that it is music which connects the rational and non-rational part of us.

[84] *The Discourses of Epictetus*, trans. P. E. Matheson (New York: Random House, 1957), 224. In another place, p. 372, he says, "for it is being a child to be unmusical in musical things, ungrammatical in grammar."

[85] Aristide' discussion begins Book II. Our quotations are from the translation by Andrew Barker, *Greek Musical Writings* (Cambridge: Cambridge University Press, 1989), II, 457ff.

[86] Cicero, *Tusculan Disputations*, II, 47.

What else is it that binds together the parts of the soul and body of man himself, who, as Aristotle is pleased to put it, has been joined together of the rational and the irrational.[87]

We find an extraordinary insight by the philosopher known as Pico in 1519.

> The intellect does not permit any lower faculty to function in collaboration with it. Rather, whenever anything comes near the intellect and arouses it, the intellect, like a roaring fire, burns it up, and converts it into itself.[88]

He was quite correct: the left hemisphere of our brain tends to completely ignore the mute right hemisphere. The implications of this have had a dramatic influence on civilization. Consider only the fact that the left hemisphere consists primarily of second-hand information; it is not the real us. Yet it tends to ignore the *real* us, the experiential right hemisphere.

Early poets writing of love often found themselves having to sing of both hemispheres, as if they realized that the emotions were fundamentally apart from language. A striking example is found in Dante (1265–1321), who, in the introduction to one of his sonnets, clearly seems aware of the separation of faculties.

> In this sonnet I make two parts of myself in accordance with the way in which my thoughts were divided. One I call *heart*, that is desire; the other *soul*, that is reason; and I relate what one says to the other.[89]

And, when Reason does speak to Desire, it makes reference to the power of the emotions to shut down Reason.

[87] Aurelian of Reome, *The Discipline of Music*, trans. Joseph Ponte (Colorado Springs: Colorado College Music Press, 1968), III. The Aristotle reference is apparently to the *Nicomachean Ethics*, I, 13.

[88] Giovanni Pico della Mirandola, *Commentary on a Canzone of Benivieni*, Sears Jayne, trans. (New York: Peter Lang, 1984), 148.

[89] *Vita Nuova*, trans. Mark Musa (Oxford: Oxford University Press, 1992), 76.

Who is this one
that comes with consolation for our mind
and who, possessing such outrageous strength,
will not allow another thought to stay?[90]

[90] Ibid., 77.

This must have been impressive, if confusing, to Dante—
that feeling could so overpower Reason. In one poem he
observes that Love overcomes the intellect like a ray of sunlight
overcoming eyes that are weak.[91] He returns to this idea twice
in the *Divine Comedy*, a reference at the beginning of *Paradise*
again using his terms of desire and intellect.

[91] "Amor che ne la mente mi ragiona,"
lines 59–60, in Frederick Goldin, *German
and Italian Lyrics of the Middle Ages*
(Garden City: Anchor Books, 1973), 377.

As it approaches its desire,
Our intellect submerges so profoundly
That our memory is unable to go back.[92]

[92] *Paradise*, I.

In the *Inferno*, he speaks of other emotions which have the same
power over the intellect.

Who could ever tell, even in straight prose,
The full story of the blood and of the wounds
That I now saw, often though it be told?
Certainly every tongue would falter, for
Neither our speech nor our intellect
Is capable of encompassing so much.[93]

[93] *Inferno*, XXVIII.

These passages demonstrate that he was clearly aware that
there is more to man than Reason.

Another early example of one who was aware of the separate
faculties was Geoffrey Chaucer (1340–1400), who, in his "The
Romaunt of the Rose," observes,

You must both perceive *and* feel that pride is a sin.[94]

[94] Lines

Later in the Renaissance we find the same kind of thought by
Guarini (1538–1612),

My heart and thoughts till now were so much set
To train that foolish nymph into my net.[95]

His Spanish contemporary, Cervantes, also recognized love's difficulty in communication,

Auristela finished her speech and began to weep tears that undid and erased everything she'd just said.[96]

Juan Vives, in his famous book, *On Education* of 1531, was not only clearly aware of the separate functions of Reason and emotions in the brain, but believed that Reason needed help and understanding in order to hold its own against the emotions.

All the precepts of Moral Philosophy have been prepared, like an army, to bring support to Reason. Wherefore the whole man must be understood, from within and without. Within the mind are the intellect and the emotions. We must know by what things the emotions are aroused and developed; by what things on the other hand they are restrained, calmed, removed ...

Our intellect is enveloped by too dense a darkness for it to see through, for the passions, aroused through sin, have spread a great and most obscuring mist before the eyes of Reason. Reason has need of being clear, and of being as little perturbed as possible.[97]

The problem in trying to have the left hemisphere speak about love (found in the right hemisphere), something it knows nothing about, of course reflects the independent nature of the two hemispheres. One frequently finds references such as one by Erasmus, who noticed that "when someone is chattering away, one can not listen to the lute."[98] Similarly, Martin Luther used to complain about his little son, Hans, singing while he was trying to write.[99]

Here are some examples of recognition of the separate hemispheres found in English literature of the Renaissance.

[95] Giambattista Guarini, *The Faithful Shepherd* [*Il Pastor Fido*], in *Five Italian Renaissance Comedies* (New York: Penguin Books, 1978), IV, 373.

[96] Miguel de Cervantes, *The Trials of Persiles and Sigismunda,* trans. Celia Weller and Clark Colahan (Berkeley: University of California Press, 1989), II, v.

[97] Foster Watson, trans., *Vives: On Education* (Cambridge: University Press, 1913), V, iii.

[98] "The Tongue," in *The Collected Works of Erasmus* (Toronto: University of Toronto Press, 1992), XXIX, 279.

[99] In a conversation of 1532 reported by Veit Dietrich, in, *Luther's Works* (St. Louis: Concordia, 1961), LIV, 21. A comment in the same conversation reveals that Luther understood the left hemisphere knew no emotions. See Ibid., 83.

Robert Greene (1560–1592):
    Can wisdom win the field, when Love is Captain?[100]

John Lyly (1554–1606):
    I cannot tell what reason it should be,
    But love and reason here do disagree.[101]

William Shakespeare:
    Ask me no reason why I love you; for though Love use
Reason for his physician, he admits him not for his counselor.[102]

The accumulation of centuries of common observation resulted in a considerable increase in discussion of the bicameral mind during the Baroque. In addition to the difficulty of communication of feelings through the rational left hemisphere of the brain, the great German philosopher Gottfried Leibniz (1646–1716) added the problem the rational side often has in describing the senses themselves.

> Additional simple primitive terms are all those confused phenomena of the senses which we certainly perceive clearly, but which we cannot explain distinctly, neither define them through other concepts, nor designate them by words.[103]

He struggled with the problem of how the rational mind could have the "idea," that is, a rational understanding, of something like emotion.[104] In the end, being a highly rational person himself (a mathematician) he fell back on the old principle that the Reason must rule.

> The highest perfection of man consists not merely in that he acts freely but still more in that he acts with reason. Better, these are both the same thing, for the less anyone's use of reason is disturbed by the impulsion of the affections, the freer one is.[105]

His great contemporary, the French philosopher, Marin Mersenne (1588–1648), speculated on the differing nature of rational and non-rational vocal sounds, that is, the difference

[100] Arbasto: *The Anatomy of Fortune* (1584), in *The Life and Complete Works of Robert Greene*, Alexander Grosart, ed. (New York: Russell & Russell, 1964), III, 197.

[101] John Lyly, *The Maydes Metamorphosis*, IV, i.

[102] *The Merry Wives of Windsor*, II, i, 4.

[103] Leibniz, "An Analysis of the Elements of Language," in *General Investigations Concerning the Analysis of Concepts and Truths*, trans. Walter O'Briant (Athens: University of Georgia Press, 1968), 33.

[104] Leibniz, "What is an Idea?" (1678), in Leroy Loemker, *Philosophical Papers and Letters* (Dordrecht: Reidel, 1956), 207.

[105] Leibniz, "Critical Thoughts on the General Part of the Principles of Descartes (1692), "On Article 37," in Ibid., 388.

between speech and singing. He wonders what would be
the nature of speech if a child were reared in an environment
which it never heard another human talk, although he doubts
such an experiment could ever be made.[106] After much speculation he concludes that the different voices which express
"the passions of the soul" in men and animals are natural, but
language itself is artificial.[107] This eventually leads him, in
Proposition 12, to wonder if "the musician can invent the best
language of all those by which the conceptions of the mind can
be expressed."[108]

The Frenchman, Blaise Pascal (1623–1662), a brilliant thinker
and inventor, seems to have been clearly aware of a bicameral
division in the mind and one of his expressions of this is a
familiar and widely quoted maxim,

> The heart has its reason, which reason does not know. We feel it
> in a thousand things.[109]

However, he incorrectly pursues the wrong road by describing
the two as the mathematical mind and the intuitive mind.
Nevertheless, here is a nice attempt to personify the two sides
as he understood them.

> Thus it is rare that mathematicians are intuitive, and that men
> of intuition are mathematicians, because mathematicians
> wish to treat matters of intuition mathematically, and make
> themselves ridiculous, wishing to begin with definitions and
> then with axioms, which is not the way to proceed in this kind
> of reasoning ...
>   Intuitive minds, on the contrary, being thus accustomed
> to judge at a single glance, are so astonished when they are
> presented with propositions of which they understand nothing,
> and the way to which is through definitions and axioms so
> sterile, and which they are not accustomed to see thus in detail,
> that they are repelled and disheartened.[110]

It is interesting that he attempts to further subdivide the
rational mind into two sections.

[106] Now such examples have been found, and such children cannot utter intelligible sounds.

[107] Marin Mersenne, *Treatise Three, Book One, Traitez de la Voix, et des Chants.*, trans. Edmund LeRoy (New York: Julliard School, unpublished dissertation, 1978), III, i, 10.

[108] There was some discussion of this during the nineteenth century and one Frenchman, François Sudre, apparently had some success in devising a "musical language."

[109] Blaise Pascal, *Pensees* (New York: Modern Library, 1941), III, 277.

[110] Ibid., I, i.

There are then two kinds of intellect: the one able to penetrate acutely and deeply into the conclusions of given premises, and this is the precise intellect; the other able to comprehend a great number of premises without confusing them, and this is the mathematical intellect.[111]

[111] Ibid., I, ii.

We find some additional interesting reflections of our bicameral mind among French writers of the Baroque, first in Charles de Saint-Evremond, in a poem contained in a letter to the Duke of Buckingham (1678), quite correctly suggests that the two hemispheres are inclined to work separately and not together.

> Sometimes let Reason, with a sovereign sway,
> Control all your desires:
> Sometimes let Reason to your heart give way,
> And fan your warmest fires.[112]

[112] Quoted in John Hayward, ed., *The Letters of Saint-Evremond* (Freeport, NY: Books for Libraries Press, 1971), 205.

Jean de La Bruyere (1645–1696) makes the same point by way of reference to separate famous French playwrights.

> The plays of Corneille occupy one's mind; those of Racine stir one's heart.[113]

[113] La Bruyere, *Characters,* trans. Jean Stewart (Baltimore: Penguin Books, 1970), 38.

At the beginning of this chapter we quoted one of La Rochefoucauld's famous maxims which reflects our bicameral mind. There are two more which perhaps should not be omitted,

> The mind is always the dupe of the heart.[114]
>   ...

[114] *The Maxims of La Rochefoucauld,* Nr. 102.

> Not all those who know their minds know their hearts as well.[115]

[115] Ibid., Nr. 103.

There are two other maxims of his which have a different focus and impress us very much. These two are relevant to the fact that the right hemisphere of our brain is mute and has no language to express itself (except through music). The first of these maxims pictures a right hemisphere communicating in a manner other than through language.

Tone of voice, look and manner can prove no less eloquent than choice of words.[116]

[116] *The Maxims of La Rochefoucauld*, op. cit., Nr. 249.

More extraordinary is his insight that there are forms of understanding unique to the right hemisphere. This is a very correct and valid truth and represents a fundamental part of us that is never approached by the field of education, since society has made the emotions "off-limits" to teachers.

Nature would seem to have hidden deep within us talents and abilities we know nothing about; only strong emotion is able to bring them to light, and to give us at times insights beyond the reach of [rational] thought.[117]

[117] Ibid., Nr. 404.

We only find one original idea of importance on our subject by the famous Descartes. This is found at the very beginning of his "Rules for the Direction of the Mind," where he contends that the hand trained for harp playing cannot be used for other pursuits, such as agriculture. All this is by way of introducing his observation that it was the arts which convinced the other intellectual disciplines that one must be a specialist in only one subject, devoting his entire life to that alone. Otherwise, he was rather a "left-brained" man, which we can see clearly in a letter of 1641 to Henricus Regius, a professor of medicine a Utrecht.

There is only one soul in man, the rational soul; for no actions can be reckoned human unless they depend on reason.

Montesquieu (1689–1755) lets the air out of this balloon with a wonderful story about a man who had been unable to sleep for thirty-five days. Ordinary physicians, at a loss, proposed to give him opium, but a friend took him to an holistic doctor (a man who "does not practice medicine, but has a multitude of remedies") who gave him a six-volume study of law. After reading a few pages, the man fell asleep.[118]

[118] Montesquieu, *The Persian Letters* (London: Athenaeum, 1901), 269.

This reminds us of another wonderful story, this one by Voltaire. His "Zadig" (1747) is a tale about a Babylonian philosopher and a wise man who "knew as much of metaphysics as hath ever been known in any age, that is, little or nothing at all." This story reflects another aspect of our bicameral mind, the fact that, as each hemisphere controls the opposite side of the body, so each eye feeds into the opposite hemisphere. Thus we must think of the right eye as the rational eye and the left as the eye dealing with our emotional life. With this in mind we return to the beginning of this story when a young man, Zadig, is wounded in the eye. A messenger is sent to Memphis for the famous physician, Hermes, who came with his large retinue. After his examination of Zadig, the doctor observed,

> Had it been the right eye, I could have cured it; but the wounds of the left eye are incurable.

In the English Baroque we find many references to our bicameral brain. Indeed, the great philosopher, David Hume (1711–1776) once noted,

> Everyone of himself will readily perceive the difference between feeling and thinking.[119]

[119] *A Treatise of Human Nature*, I, i, section 1.

In Phineas Fletcher's poem, "The Purple Island," largely a description of a city as a metaphor for a map of anatomy, we have a curious early description of the twin hemispheres of the brain surrounded by the skull.

> Here all the senses dwell, and all the arts;
> Here learned Muses by their silver spring:
> The Citie severed in two diverse parts,
> Within the walls, and Suburbs neighboring;
> The Suburbs girt but with the common fence,
> Founded with wondrous skill, and great expense;
> And therefore beautie here keeps her chief residence.[120]

[120] In Frederick Boas, *Giles and Phineas Fletcher Poetical Works* (Cambridge: University Press, 1909), II, 54.

A poem by Thomas Sheridan (1687–1738), a priest and schoolmaster, is a remarkable example of someone who had arrived at the bicameral division of the brain purely by intuition. He is absolutely, and astonishingly, correct in his assigning of right or left eye and ear functions vis-a-vis their actual relationship with the brain hemispheres. Indeed, it is difficult to believe this was written before the availability of the results of clinical brain research.

> With my left eye, I see you sit snug in your stall,
> With my right I'm attending the lawyers that scrawl.
> With my left I behold your bellower a cur chase;
> With my right I'm reading my deeds for a purchase.
> My left ear's attending the hymns of the choir,
> My right ear is stunned with the noise of the crier.[121]

121 Quoted in *The Poetical Works of Jonathan Swift* (London: Bell and Daldy, n.d.), III, 245.

Since, as most readers know today, our two hemispheres tend to work separately, and not together, according to which side is best equipped for a particular problem, we should like to include two examples of English writers complaining about the interference of one side or the other. Charles Avison (1709–1770), in one place, observes that people sing with more emotion when they visit foreign churches and cannot read the words to the hymns. His point, of course, is that in this case the right hemisphere is not hampered by the left at all.[122]

122 Charles Avison, *An Essay on Musical Expression* [London, 1753] (New York: Broude Reprint, 1967), 88.

On the other hand, so to speak, Richard Steele, in the *Spectator* for 24 September 1712, published a fictitious complaint that our emotions carry us away, whereas the sermon is soon forgotten.

> A loose trivial song gains the affections, when a wise Homily is not attended to.

For the nineteenth century we need only point to the experience of the great composers, who also made observations which reflect the recognition of the conflict between the two hemispheres of our brain. Mendelssohn, for example, once noticed that sometimes he became so emotionally involved while he was conducting that he had difficulty in maintaining the beat. In this case, we know conductors use the right hand to give the beat, as it is controlled by the left hemisphere which knows the notation and the numbers of music. When Mendelssohn became emotionally involved, his right hemisphere was interfering with the left hemisphere function. Similarly, Schumann once remarked that when he was absorbed in music he found that he had difficulty remembering his German language!

The musician who wrote most extensively on the subject of our bicameral selves was Richard Wagner and his writings are worthy of thoughtful contemplation, certainly by all musicians. Instead of using terms like left and right (which he had no knowledge of) and rational versus non-rational, he used the terms Understanding versus Feeling, which, of course, match perfectly the primary functions of the two hemispheres of our brain. He makes a number of contentions, beginning with the statement that the musician "addresses himself to Feeling, and not to Understanding."[123] And he says if the musician is answered in terms of Understanding, you might as well say he was not understood. One can see right there how shocked he would be if he could observe American music education, which aspires to do just the reverse.

He also wrote in this regard on the subject of the development of modern languages, pointing out that language must have been based on feeling but that it has developed in such a manner that today, "we speak a language we do not understand with the Feeling [side]."[124] On the other hand, he contends that poetry is impossible unless it passes "from the Understanding to the Feeling."[125]

In addition, his attempts to write of music theory in terms of feeling,[126] is certainly a foreign concept in modern classrooms. In our view his explanation is not so successful here, but in making the effort he creates a wonderfully romantic discussion of this left-brain topic which is very refreshing.

[123] William Ashton Ellis, ed., *Wagner's Prose Works* (New York: Broude, I, 270ff.

[124] Ibid., II, 230.

[125] Ibid., II, 232.

[126] Ibid., II, 291.

On Emotion and Music

Music is a special language for the communication of feelings and emotion to the listener.

MUSIC IS DISTINCT FROM THE OTHER ARTS in many ways, but in no way more fundamental than in its unique synthesis with the physiology of man. Not only did early man hear the overtone series in every sound he heard and depend on pitch awareness for survival, but recent research has established that every organ of his body produced a specific pitch. In addition, all philologists agree that some form of music, sung vowel-like expressions of basic emotions, preceded the earliest speech and was man's first form of oral communication. We carry this genetically, as we still invest every sentence we speak with musical contour. In the previous essay the reader saw the long history of the recognition of our bicameral brain and it is the very physiology of the brain that provides music with its great power to express what the rational mind cannot. And this is why the definition of music given above is probably the definition most people would understand, even the common uneducated masses.

The ancient writers also clearly recognized the fact that the ability to appreciate and understand music is not dependent on any technical knowledge whatsoever. Petrarch, for example, quotes Cicero as saying the music "tickles their ears, without their knowing why."[127] It is remarkable that an almost

[127] Letter to Boccaccio, in James Robinson, *Petrarch, The First Modern Scholar and Man of Letters* (New York: Putnam, 1914), 184.

identical statement was made by Mozart in a letter to his father,

> These passages are written in such a way that the less learned cannot fail to be pleased, though without knowing why.[128]

[128] December 28, 1782.

With the beginning of the Christian Era, the construction of concert halls, private and public concerts of art music, together with popular music and sung poetry, all continued, although one would never discover this in reading music history texts which describe the Middle Ages. There was, however, a new development which had far reaching consequences in music practice. The new Christian Church, consumed with the desire to rid Western Europe of all things "pagan," took a very strong stand against all expression of emotions. Emotions, the Church fathers proclaimed, were the path to sin. St. Basil even proposed that the proper Christian should not even laugh, because nowhere in the New Testament is Jesus described as laughing.

The Church recognized only the rational side of man and when the first important music treatises began to appear they followed this same line. As a result, when the first universities began to be established, music was placed in the faculty of mathematics and all music courses were taught by, and music treatises written by, mathematicians. This association of music with math and Reason, rather than with emotions and the experiential side of man, remains very much a part of music instruction to the present day. Modern music schools continue to teach a great deal of math. Rhythm, for example, is taught exclusively as math, resulting in the inability of our students to *feel* rhythm.

It was only the rediscovery and publication of the ancient Greek treatises which led to the rejection of the old Church nonsense about music and restored an understanding of the true nature of music. It was this Renaissance movement which we call Humanism. We might let a definition by Galilei, in 1581, very similar to the one we have given above, represent this broad and powerful return to the values of the ancient Greeks. "True music," he wrote, has a primary purpose "to express the passions" and, secondarily, "to communicate these with equal force to the minds of mortals for their benefit and advantage."[129] Certainly in no medieval music treatise does one find a statement such as this one by Martin Luther: "Only music deserves being extolled as the mistress and governess of the feelings of the human heart."[130]

The university treatises of the Renaissance still speak of music as being math, but here and there a writer lets down his academic guard and reveals a world of change. Heinrich Glarean, in his *Dodecachordon* (1547) for example, a treatise heavily focused on the technical aspects of music, nevertheless reveals the depth of emotion he himself experienced as a listener of actual performance. He mentions hearing an "Elegy of Magdalene," by Michael de Verona, which he heard as,

> possessing great emotion and innate sweetness and tremendous power, so that one really believes he hears the weeping of a woman ... At the end, through a certain confident hope, it rises so magnificently and is lifted to the heights with such tremendous exultation, and then again, as if wearied and self-reproachful for immoderate joy, it falls back into deep and customary weeping.[131]

Of all the periods of music history, none has been more inaccurately portrayed by musicologists than the Renaissance. Music history texts give the impression that Church music *was* Renaissance music, whereas in fact there was a great deal more than that. A composer such as Machaut would have been utterly astonished if he could have known that he would be remembered today for his Church music, an insignificant proportion of his music upon which he placed little value in comparison to his love songs. It is also because scholars concentrate only on Church music, that we never read that the people who actually knew Leonardo da Vinci considered him the greatest *musician* they knew. And why have these same books

[129] Oliver Strunk, *Source Readings in Music History* (New York: Norton, 1950), 306ff.

[130] Luther, Preface to a collection of part-songs (1538) based on the suffering and death of Jesus.

[131] Glarean, *Dodecachordon*, trans. Clement Miller (American Institute of Musicology, 1965), II, 258ff.

kept from us descriptions of such powerful performances of art music as that by Francesco da Milano in 1555?

> He made the very strings to swoon beneath his fingers and transported all who listened into such gentle melancholy that one present buried his head in his hands, another let his entire body slump into an ungainly posture with members all awry, while another, his mouth sagged open and his eyes more than half shut, seemed, one would judge, as if transfixed upon the strings, and yet another, with chin sunk upon his chest, hiding the most sadly taciturn visage ever seen, remained abstracted in all his senses save his hearing, as if his soul had fled from all the seats of sensibility to take refuge in his ears where more easefully it could rejoice in such enchanting symphony.[132]

[132] Pontus de Tyard, *Solitaire second* (1555).

Who has ever read a description of listeners of Renaissance church music which compares with that? The truth of the matter is that the Church polyphony, upon which our modern music history texts are based, was music heard by the actual people living during the Renaissance as being already old-fashioned and scholastic. This was because this music was composed upon principles of mathematics, and not of feeling. For example, Pontus de Tyard, a member of the group of French poets known as the *Plaiade*, observed,

> Music's purpose seems to be that of setting the word in such a fashion that anyone listening to it will become impassioned and carried away by the mood of the poet. The musician who knows how to deploy the solo voice to this end best attains his goal, in my opinion. Contrapuntal music most often brings to the ears only a lot of noise, from which you feel no vivid effect.[133]

[133] Pontus de Tyard, *Les Discours philosophiques* (Paris, 1587).

Similarly, Zarlino wrote,

> Even in our times we see that music induces in us various passions in the way that it did in antiquity. For occasionally, it is observed, when some beautiful, learned, and elegant poem is recited by someone to the sound of some instrument, the listeners are greatly stirred and moved to do different

things, such as to laugh, weep, or to similar actions ... If such effects were wrought by music in antiquity, it was recited as described above and not in the way that is used at present, with a multitude of parts and so many singers and instruments that at times nothing is heard but a jumbled din of voices and diverse instrumental sounds, singing without taste or discretion, and an unseemly pronunciation of words, so that he hears only a tumult and uproar. Music practiced in this way cannot have any effect on us worth remembering.[134]

[134] *Le Istitutioni harmoniche*, II, ix, 75.

It was in the Renaissance, then, that Europe began to rediscover the fundamental role of the emotions in music. The story of the Baroque Era is one of an obsession for emotions in music by both composers and philosophers alike. Again, the view of the Baroque given us by musicologists over the past hundred years is so incomplete, and therefore misleading, that many musicians today do not even think of Baroque music as being emotional at heart. Many musicians have been misled by their teachers into thinking of Baroque music as math, now called counterpoint and functional-bass chord progressions.

But the better Baroque composers never talked like that! Cavalieri, in the preface to his *La rappresentatione di Anima* (1600) says his goal is to "move listeners to different emotions, such as pity and joy, tears and laughter."[135] And Caccini, in his *Le Nuove Musiche*, writes that the goal of his solo songs was "to move the affect of the soul."[136] Speaking of his *Il Gran Tamerlano* (1706), Scarlatti relates that he tried to achieve, "naturalness and beauty, together with the expression of the passion."[137] And Karl Philipp Emanuel Bach wrote,

[135] Quoted in Nino Pirrotta and Elena Povoledo, *Music and Theatre from Poliziano to Monteverdi* (Cambridge: Cambridge University Press, 1982), 241.
[136] *Le Nuove Musiche*, 45.

[137] Quoted in Claude Palisca, *Baroque Music* (Englewood Cliffs: Prentice Hall, 1981), 236ff.

> It appears to me that it is the special province of music to move the heart.[138]

[138] Quoted in Nat Shapiro, *An Encyclopedia of Quotations About Music* (New York: Da Capo, 1978), 192.

We might also add that in his biographical work, *Ehrenpforte* (Hamburg, 1740), in reference to a person who had claimed both a goal of making "music a scientific or scholarly pursuit" and an association with J. S. Bach, Johann Mattheson adds that Bach certainly did not teach this man "the supposed mathematical basis of composition." "This," Mattheson testifies, "I can guarantee."[139]

Even the music theorists of the Baroque were no longer talking only about mathematics. Their enthusiasm was for writing of the "affections" and the "passions." It was now very clear that the composer was driven by emotions, and not by mathematics. Charles Butler wrote, in 1636,

> [Good composing is impossible] unless the Author, at the time of Composing, be transported as it were with some Musical fury; so that himself scarce knoweth what he doth, nor can presently give a reason for his doing.[140]

Angelo Berardi wrote in 1681 that "Music is the ruler of the passions of the soul."[141] Even Marin Mersenne, who attempted in his great encyclopedia to explain all of music by mathematics, was forced in his most concise definition of music to admit that song,

> is a derivation of the voice, or of other sounds, by certain intervals either natural or artificial, which are agreeable to the ear and to the spirit, and which signify joy, or sadness, or some other passion by their movements.[142]

It is at this time also that we find philosophers focusing on the emotions when writing of the purpose of music. Even that left-brained, mechanically obsessed, Descartes, in his definition of music, had to admit,

> The basis of music is sound; its aim is to please and to arouse various emotions in us.[143]

William Temple emphasized the genetic universality of the emotions in music.

> The powers of music are either felt or known by all men, and are allowed to work strangely upon the mind and the body, the

[139] Quoted in Hans T. David and Arthur Mendel, *The Bach Reader* (New York: Norton, 1966), 440.

[140] Charles Butler, *The Principles of Musik in Singing and Setting* [1636] (New York: Da Capo Press, 1970), 92.

[141] Angelo Berardi, *Ragionamenti Musicali* (Bologna, 1681), 87.

[142] Marin Mersenne, *Harmonie universelle*, Treatise Three, Book Two ("Second Book of Songs") *of the Traitez de la Voix et des Chants ...*, trans. Wilbur F. Russell (Princeton: Westminster Choir College, unpublished dissertation, 1952), III, ii, 1.

[143] *Compendium of Music*, Walter Robert, trans. (American Institute of Musicology, 1961), 11.

passions and the blood; to raise joy and grief, to give pleasure and pain, to cure diseases and the mortal sting of the tarantula; to give motions to the feet as well as the heart, to compose disturbed thoughts, to assist and heighten devotion itself.[144]

[144] "Of Poetry," in *Five Miscellaneous Essays by Sir William Temple*, ed. Samuel Monk (Ann Arbor: University of Michigan Press, 1963), 177.

Seventeenth-century poets also frequently wrote of the emotions in music. A remarkable example is Dryden's *A Song for St. Cecilia's Day*, 1687. After an initial burst of enthusiasm, "What Passion cannot Musick raise and quell!," he presents a remarkable survey of the emotional qualities which he associates with various musical instruments. It is imagery worthy of Berlioz.

> The TRUMPETS loud clangor
> Excites us to arms
> With shrill notes of anger ...
> .....
> The soft complaining FLUTE
> In dying Notes discovers
> The woes of hopeless lovers,
> Whose dirge is whispered by the warbling LUTE.
> .....
> Sharp VIOLINS proclaim
> Their jealous pangs, and desperation,
> Fury, frantick indignation,
> Depth of pains, and height of passion.

But the real evidence for the consuming interest in the emotions among Baroque musicians is found in the contemporary descriptions of their performance. To begin with singers, Severo Bonini has left this description of the singing of one of the first opera composers.

> A much learned singer and composer was Signor Jacopo Peri, who would have moved and brought to tears the hardest heart by singing his works.[145]

[145] Quoted in Nino Pirrotta and Elena Povoledo, op. cit., 246.

And consider the range of emotions mentioned by Christoph Bernhard, in his singing treatise of 1649.

In the recitative style, one should take care that the voice is raised in moments of anger, and to the contrary dropped in moments of grief. Pain makes it pause; impatience hastens it. Happiness enlivens it. Desire emboldens it. Love renders it alert. Bashfulness holds it back. Hope strengthens it. Despair diminishes it. Fear keeps it down. Danger is fled with screams. If, however, a person faces up to danger, then his voice must reflect his daring and bravery.[146]

[146] Quoted in Ellen Harris, "Voices," in *Performance Practice: Music after 1600* (New York: Norton, 1989), 110.

Tosi, although writing a treatise on vocal technique, was never so passionate as when he spoke of "heart."

Oh! how great a master is the heart! Confess it, my beloved singers, and gratefully admit, that you would not have arrived at the highest rank of the profession if you had not been its scholars.[147]

[147] P. F. Tosi, *Observations on the Florid Song* (London: Wilcox, 1743), IX, xliv.

A manuscript by Diderot describes the nephew of Rameau as an amateur singing in a cafe.

While singing fragments of Jomelli's *Lamentations*, he reproduced with incredible precision, fidelity, and warmth the most beautiful passages of each scene. In that magnificent recitative in which Jeremiah describes the desolation of Jerusalem he was drenched in tears, which drew their like from every onlooker. His art was complete—delicacy of voice, expressive strength, true sorrow …

Worn out, exhausted, like a man emerging from a deep sleep or a prolonged reverie, he stood motionless, dumb, petrified. He kept looking around him like a man who has lost his way and wants to know where he is. He waited for returning strength and wits, wiping his face with an absent-minded gesture.[148]

[148] Quoted in *Rameau's Nephew and Other Works*, trans. Jacques Barzun (Garden City: Doubleday, 1956), 69.

The most dramatic descriptions of Baroque performers are those of violinists, such as this one heard by a French critic in 1702, as,

an ecstatic who was so carried away with the piece that he was playing that he not only martyred his instrument but also himself. No longer master of his own being, he became so transported that he gyrated and hopped around like someone overcome by a demon.[149]

The critic, François Raguenet, describes another.

> The artist himself, whilst he is performing it, is seized with an unavoidable agony; he tortures his violin; he racks his body; he is no longer master of himself, but is agitated like one possessed with an irresistible motion.[150]

If there is still a reader anywhere who is under the impression that Baroque music was mechanical and boring, perhaps this eyewitness description of the famous Corelli will make him wonder if he has been misinformed.

> I never met with any man that suffered his passions to hurry him away so much whilst he was playing on the violin as the famous Arcangelo Corelli, whose eyes will sometimes turn as red as fire; his countenance will be distorted, his eyeballs roll as in an agony, and he gives in so much to what he is doing that he doth not look like the same man.[151]

In some cases, accounts by contemporary listeners suggest an emotional impact much greater than we might experience in hearing the same music today. The English actor, Betterton, found,

> Purcell penetrates the heart, makes the blood dance through your veins, and thrill with the agreeable violence offered by his Heavenly Harmony.[152]

And consider the impact of mere incidental music in a play, as recalled by Pepys, in a February 27, 1668, entry in his famous *Diary*.

> What did please me beyond anything in the whole world was the wind-musique when the Angel comes down, which is so

[149] Quoted in Hans-Peter Schmitz, *Die Kunst der Verzierung im 18. Jahrhundert* (Kassel: Barenreiter, 1955), 12.

[150] François Raguenet, "Parallele des Italiens et des Français," (1702), quoted in Strunk, op. cit., 478ff.

[151] O. Strunk, François Raguenet, *Comparison between the French and Italian Music* (1702), in *The Musical Quarterly* XXXII (1946), 419fn.

[152] Charles Gildon, *The Life of Mr. Thomas Betterton, the Late Eminent Tragedian* [1710] (London: Frank Cass Reprint, 1970), 155ff.

sweet that it ravished me; and indeed, in a word, did wrap up
my soul so that it make me really sick, just as I have formerly
been when in love with my wife; that neither then, nor all
the evening going home and at home, I was able to think of
anything, but remained all night transported, so as I could not
believe that ever any music has that real command over the soul
of a man as this did upon me; and makes me resolve to practice
wind-music and to make my wife do the same.

One vivid portrait of an attentive audience is found in a
description of a performance of Handel.

The audience was so enchanted with this performance, that a
stranger who should have seen the manner in which they were
affected, would have imagined they had all been distracted.[153]

Such a description of the distracted minds of the listeners
was also mentioned in 1690 by James Talbot, who found the
Sarabande soft and passionate in character, "apt to move the
Passions and to disturb the tranquility of the Mind."[154]

Finally, there is this rather remarkable advice to the listener by
Rameau, himself famous during his lifetime as a theoretician.

Often we think we hear in music only what exists in the words,
or in the interpretation we wish to give them. We try to subject
music to forced inflections, but that is not the way to be able to
judge it. On the contrary, we must not think but let ourselves be
carried away by the feeling which the music inspires; without
our thinking at all, this feeling will become the basis of our
judgment.[155]

The strong focus on the emotions demonstrated in Italian
opera helped prepare the melodically expressive music of the
Classic Period. Equally significant was the influence of the
Enlightenment which encouraged even the Catholic composers
to write music which expressed their own feelings, instead of
thinking of themselves as surrogates for God. Thus in Friedrich
Marpurg's view in 1750,

[153] J. Mainwaring, *Memoirs of Handel* (1760), quoted in Robert Donnington, *The Interpretation of Early Music* (New York, 1964), 96.

[154] Quoted in Ibid., 402.

[155] Jean Philippe Rameau, *Observations sur notre instinct pour la musique et sur son principe.*

The composer's task is to copy nature ... to stir the passions at will ... to express the living movements of the soul and the cravings of the heart.[156]

[156] *Der Critische Musicus an der Spree* (1750), I.

Now, in expressing emotions, the composers no longer sought the exaggeration of the Baroque, and Italian opera in particular, but instead sought to express more natural and true emotions. Thus, Mozart, describing his *Die Entfuhrung aus dem Serail* for his father, wrote,

Now, as for Belmonte's aria in A major, do you know how it is expressed—even the throbbing of his loving heart is indicated— the two violins in octaves ... One sees the trembling—the wavering—one sees how his swelling breast heaves—this is expressed by a crescendo—one hears the whispering and the sighing—which is expressed by the first violins, muted, and a flute in unison. Nothing could be more definite than that.[157]

[157] Letter to his father, September 26, 1781.

And it is no surprise to find Mozart complimenting Mlle. Weber's singing, by remarking that her singing "goes to the heart."[158]

[158] Letter to his father, February 19, 1778.

From this time until the twentieth century, no one questioned the fact that the paramount role of music was to express the emotions. When Beethoven finished his *Missa Solemnis,* he wrote on the score, "From the heart, may it go to the heart." Subsequent composers clearly made the expression of emotions through music their credo. Consider the following:

Schumann:
   Music is to me the perfect expression of the soul.[159]

[159] Letter to his mother, Leipzig, May 8, 1832.

Berlioz:
   The prevailing characteristics of my music are passionate expression, intense ardor, rhythmical animation, and unexpected turns.[160]

[160] *Memoirs.*

Chopin:
   A long time ago I decided that my universe will be the soul and heart of man.[161]

[161] Letter to Delphine Potocka. Chopin's last words were reported to be, "Play Mozart in memory of me."

Verdi:

   I should compose with utter confidence a subject that set my blood going, even though it were condemned by all other artists as anti-musical.[162]

[162] Letter of 1854.

Mahler:

   What is best in music is not to be found in the notes.[163]

[163] A frequent observation by Mahler, according to Bruno Walter, *Gustav Mahler* (New York: Greystone Press, 1941), 83.

Paul Dukas:

   Be it laughter or tears, feverish passion or religious ecstasy, nothing, in the category of human feelings, is a stranger to music.[164]

[164] Quoted in Nat Shapiro, op. cit., 194.

Max Reger:

   Music, in and by itself, should generate a flow of pure emotion without the least tinge of extraneous rationalization.[165]

[165] Letter to Adalbert Lindner (June 6, 1891)

Ravel:

   Music, I feel, must be emotional first and intellectual second.[166]

[166] Quoted in Nat Shapiro, op. cit., 197.

Frederick Delius:

   Music is an outburst of the soul.[167]

[167] Ibid., 11.

Because it was so evident that the purpose of music was to express emotion, over a long period of time some philosophers had been speaking of music as an actual language of the emotions. Already in the sixteenth century, Martin Luther had observed, "Music is a language of feelings without words."[168] Subsequent philosophers in France, Descartes, Chénier, Nodier, Chabanon, De Vismes and J.-J. Rousseau in particular, began to speculate on the possibility of an international language based on music which might replace traditional languages. The extraordinary attempts of Jean-François Sudre to realize this dream with his *"Langue Musicale Universelle"* had no successor, with the exception of Wagner, who almost certainly found his *leitmotif* concept here.

[168] Luther, Preface to Rhau's *Symphoniae iucundae* (1538).

Some other familiar persons commented on the idea of music as a language, among them,

Mendelssohn:

People usually complain that music is so ambiguous; that it is so doubtful what they ought to think when they hear it; whereas everyone understands words. With me it is entirely the reverse. And not only with regard to an entire speech, but also with individual words; these, too, seem to me to be so ambiguous, so vague, and so easily misunderstood in comparison with genuine music, which fills the soul with a thousand things better than words. The thoughts which are expressed to me by a piece of music which I love are not too indefinite to be put into words, but on the contrary too definite.[169]

[169] Letter to Marc André Souchay (October 5, 1842).

Moussorgsky:

Music is a means of communicating with people, not an aim in itself.

Edward MacDowell:

Music ... is a language, but a language of the intangible, a kind of soul-language.[170]

[170] *Critical and Historical Essays* (1912).

Wagner:

Music is the speech of Passion.[171]

.....

It is a truth forever, that where the speech of man stops short, there Music's reign begins.[172]

[171] Wagner, "Judaism in Music."

[172] Wagner, "A Happy Evening."

Hans Christian Anderson:

Where words fail, music speaks.

Leo Tolstoy:

Music is the shorthand of emotion. Emotions which let themselves be described in words with such difficulty, are directly conveyed to man in music, and in that is its power and significance.[173]

[173] Quoted in Nat Shapiro, op. cit., 199.

Bruno Walter:

At no time and in no place has music been merely playing with sounds. The vibrations themselves which we perceive as musical sounds are not exclusively material in nature—affective elements are active in them, lending inner meaning and coherence to the sound phenomenon: only thus can the successive and simultaneous arrangement of notes become a musical language whose eloquence speaks to the human soul.[174]

[174] Bruno Walter, *Of Music and Music-Making* (New York: Norton, 1957), 65.

Comments regarding emotions and music by 19th century performers are also very numerous. Among them we find,

Carl Junker, on Beethoven as pianist,

He is more for the heart.[175]

[175] Bossler's *Musikalische Correspondenz* (November 23, 1791).

Clara Schumann, on Brahms,

It is really moving to see him sitting at the piano, with his interesting young face which becomes transfigured when he plays.[176]

[176] Clara Schumann, *Diary* (September, 1853). Wagner, curiously, found Brahms not expressive enough: The execution of Herr Brahms appeared so painfully dry, inflexible and wooden. I should have liked to see Herr Brahms's technique anointed with a little of the oil of Liszt's school. ["Treatise on Conducting"]

Arthur Rubinstein:

When I play, I make love—it is the same thing.[177]

[177] *Arthur Rubinstein: Love of Life* (film, 1975).

Listeners during the nineteenth century had become fully conditioned to hear music as a synonymous expression of feeling. From an endless supply of possible quotations, consider only these two remarkable testimonies to the experience of hearing the music of Mozart.

Tchaikovsky:
Here are things which can bring tears to our eyes. I will only mention the adagio of the D minor string quintet. No one else has ever known as well how to interpret so exquisitely in music the sense of resigned and inconsolable sorrow. Every time Laub played the adagio I had to hide in the farthest corner of the concert-room, so that others might not see how deeply this music affected me.[178]

[178] Letter to von Meck, March 16, 1878.

Sšren Kierkegaard:

    I am in love with Mozart like a young girl. Immortal Mozart!
I owe you everything; it is thanks to you that I lost my reason,
that my soul was awestruck in the very depths of my being ... I
have you to thank that I did not die without having loved.[179]

179 *Either/Or* (1843).

Three thousand years of experience were not enough to
discourage radical new departures during the twentieth
century. One new school of composers championed "objective"
music, which had never ever existed before. Their credo was
that music can be understood only as C♯s and B♭s, and some
significant voices attempted to make their case.

Stravinsky:

    I consider that music is, by its very nature, powerless to
express anything at all, whether a feeling, an attitude of mind,
a psychological mood, a phenomenon of nature, etc ... If, as is
nearly always the case, music appears to express something, this
is only an illusion, and not a reality.[180]

180 *Chronicle of My Life* (English edition),
91ff.

Hindemith:

    Music cannot express the composer's feelings.[181]

181 *A Composer's World.*

Actually, of course, such composers as Stravinsky and Hindemith wrote some very emotionally expressive music, their
above comments notwithstanding, for the simple reason that
they could not avoid being human, that is, sharing the universal emotions of all mankind. For the most part, however, the
composers of "objective" music found their greatest admir-
ers and followers among the academic community and not
among the general public, who never responded as it did for
traditional music. For the general public there is not a single
work from this school which communicates as directly as the
weakest Beethoven symphony.

We might include under the caption of "objective" music a
considerable amount of educational music. Perhaps a more
accurate caption might be "the publisher's objective" music,
for this music often seems "constructed to measure" and not

inspired. Why, we wonder, would we wish to give children music which is not inspired?

The twelve-tone school was, of course, a return to math, in so far as the process was concerned. This school is now completely dead and nearly forgotten. It lasted exactly as long as the Classic Period, which produced numerous masterpieces which will be performed forever. How many compositions from the seventy-five years of twelve-tone music will be performed forever? One can count them on one hand.

Another significant new influence of the twentieth century has been the recording industry, which has made technical accuracy a higher goal than feeling. The impact of this influence can be clearly seen in the criticism of the later recordings by Karajan. Peter Davis, in New York Magazine, called Karajan,

> master of the recorded cult which has purged the spirit from the music.

A senior British critic considered the absence of feeling in a Karajan performance of the Beethoven Eroica as amounting to fraud.

> Beauty without form, sound without meaning, power without reason, reason without soul—it is the deadly logic of hi-fi. Machines, we are told, will one day compose symphonies. At present they merely perform them.

Some fear bands have been similarly influenced, resulting in concerts which are characterized by great demonstrations of technical skill and precision but lacking in genuine feeling.

On Aesthetics

Does it matter what we program and perform?

> Never play bad compositions and never listen to them when not absolutely obliged to do so.
>   .....
> You ought not help to spread bad compositions, but, on the contrary, help to suppress them with all your force.
> —Robert Schumann, *Maxims for Young Musicians*

ON THE FINAL DAY of my 2017 conducting tour of Italy I took advantage of a rare non-professional day to visit the famous medieval cathedral in Milano. As I was sitting in the nave enjoying a quiet moment of contemplation following a very full five weeks of conducting and teaching seminars, not to mention the time consumed by travel itself, I began to consider my fellow visitors to this great architectural marvel.

The plaza before this cathedral is always filled with hundreds of visitors to Milano and a great many of them stand in very long lines waiting to obtain a ticket to visit the cathedral and then in additional long lines to actually enter the church. Why, I began to wonder, are these hundreds of ordinary tourists, most of whom had probably not been in any church during the past months, willing to stand an hour or more in lines to see the inside of this cathedral? To be sure, the building is prominently featured in all tourist publications as one of the things to see in Milano, but is there anything else in Milano, save the famous painting by Leonardo, for which they would make this physical sacrifice?

Once inside the great expanse of this cathedral, excepting a few in prayer, these tourists, in their shorts and baseball caps, with cell-phones and other means of photography at hand, seemed to me to be noticeably lost. Most were walking without direction, looking left and right and appearing somewhat confused about what to admire. They were taking pictures of tombs and memorial stones of obscure, long forgotten archbishops, photos of the stain glass windows of course, but mostly taking pictures of themselves—documenting their presence in this famous tourist destination.

That these people seemed lost we must attribute to the poverty of their education. Yet there was something in their background that caused them think it was important to be there. The fact is that the majority of adults who populate our audiences are much like these people in Milano. They are very poorly educated in aesthetic music and worse they have been subjected to the lowest possible popular music. Yet they see a concert advertized and something tells them it would be worth going to the trouble of going to hear it.

The conductor, more than anyone else, holds the key to whether it will be worthwhile or not. Has the conductor given this any thought? And if so, what are his choices?

First, does the public need more entertainment? Almost everyone today has access to hundreds of TV channels which are mostly entertainment in character. Then there are sport events beyond number which are available to the public. Film has become mostly comic, and in some cases actual illustrated cartoons. And if the goal of the modern concert is to supply more entertainment to the public, how can it compete with the great sums of money spent promoting commercial entertainment music?

The band could perform a great public service in bringing aesthetic repertoire to an audience which has little access to it. Instead of being one more medium which contributes to the lowering of taste, the wind band could be a medium which enlightens its public and contributes to raising the level of its taste. With aesthetic music the orchestra and wind band could provide its listeners with what Aristotle called catharsis, the experience of having music cause a deeper and lasting form of introspection. Would this not be a higher and more ethical form of public contribution than merely seeking more applause?

The nature of the performance of music and its impact on the feelings of the listener is what music is all about. While this is generally ignored by writings on music history, it is the very central core of writings on the Aesthetics of Music. Aesthetics, as a separate branch of philosophy, was founded by Aristotle in his famous book, *Poetics*. In this book, intended as a kind of textbook for those playwrights wishing to write Tragedy, Aristotle in his careful step-by-step manner discusses the various fundamental parts of Tragedy, such as character, time restrictions of the plot, style of language, etc. But when he was finished he realized that there was something left—the nature of the impact on the listener. He found that some stage plays reached deeply inside the observer, even changing his behavior. Other plays, while engaging while on the stage, only seemed to "bounce off" the listener and made no lasting impression. Thus he distinguished between the Aesthetic and Entertainment, and this distinction continued to be acknowledged by philosophers for the next two thousand years.

If the purpose is to create an aesthetic concert, then the primary purpose of the conductor is to know the music. But where does he find it? The eyes cannot help, for music is not found on the page, only the grammar. Everyone knows the famous remark by Mahler that the important things about music are not found in the notes. Music is a special language for communicating emotions between composer and listener. Since both emotions and the experiential nature of music are found only in the composer's right hemisphere of the brain, it follows that that is where we must find the music. But the right hemisphere is mute, it cannot write or speak. We are left, then, with the notes the composer wrote on paper. These notes are not music. As Aristotle made very clear 2,500 years ago, things written on paper are only symbols of the real thing and not the real thing itself. This is the literal meaning of Mahler's comment; these notes are not music.

The purpose of the conductor, therefore, is not to conduct these notes, but to conduct that which they are only symbols of. But where can a conductor look to find what is behind the notes? To begin with the conductor has the score, which in addition to the symbols written on paper, is also a key to the composer's mind. Another place to look, in my own experience, has been with the eyes closed. This is where memorization pays off. If you know the music as it appears on paper well enough that you can sit down, close your eyes and listen in your head to the performance of a composition from beginning to end, it always turns out that important new insights will present themselves, things which could not be put on paper. It is in this context that I always recall a famous Sufi parable.

A student was walking through the village, whereupon he came to the house of his teacher. There he saw his teacher, on his hands and knees in his yard, apparently looking for something in the grass.

"Master, what are you looking for?"

"I am looking for my house key," his teacher replied, "Come and help me look for it!"

The student joined his teacher in the grass, but after a time he concluded that there was probably no key in the grass at all and that this was intended to be some sort of lesson.

"OK, Master, where did you actually lose your house key?"

His teacher answered, "Well, actually I lost it somewhere inside my house."

"Why then," said the student, "are we looking out here in the grass?"

"Because there is more light here," explained the teacher.

Whether from the perspective of science or philosophy, it is clear that we are a bicameral species. We have a rational side, which involves most of the common activities of life, and an experiential side, which involves only our own personal experiences, feelings and emotions and awareness of our senses. Almost all of education is designed for the rational side, and is, incidentally, entirely past tense. Because our experiential side is entirely personal in nature, and is the real present tense us, there is a kind of void with respect to the world of facts and data of which most of society depends. It is this void which causes a certain insecurity in one's cognizance of his own spiritual life. Adding to this insecurity is the fact that our experiential side, the right hemisphere of our brain, is mute, it cannot write or speak. It is the consequence of this insecurity in our spiritual awareness which, I believe, is the origin of our unconscious need for contact with the spiritual world, including both music and religion. We are drawn instinctively to both music and religion in the need for experiencing an uplifting in our spiritual life. This need for uplifting the spiritual side of ourselves, as opposed to mere entertaining or pleasing ourselves, is what Aristotle recognized when he created the new branch of philosophy, Aesthetics.

We Need to Rethink how we Teach Music

MUSIC EDUCATION IS VERY ANCIENT. Plato wrote that music education in ancient Egypt was highly organized 10,000 years before his time. That would take us back to the period of the cave painting in Spain and France, making music teaching one of the oldest professions.

That ancient music education, 13,000 years before our time was conducted on the basis of no notation. Even in the following periods of the high Greek culture during the lives of Plato and Aristotle there was still no notation; at the time of Aristotle the individual notes did not even yet have names. To them this did not in any way seem unnatural.

> In Music the ear obeys only Nature. It takes account of neither measure nor range. Instinct alone leads it.
> —Jean Philippe Rameau (1683–1764)

The greatest transformation in the long history of Music and man came with the invention of notation by the late Medieval Church to facilitate teaching boys to serve in the choir [ladies not permitted]. For the first time Music became something for the eye!

But there was something very important lost with the advent of notation. With the victory of the Roman Church over the Roman Empire in the fourth and fifth centuries, the Church set out to recreate the Roman citizen. Foremost among the Church's goals was the elimination of emotion from the lives of the new faithful, for in its view the emotions were the first step toward sin. The Church Fathers repeatedly warned against going to the theater, to music events and sporting events because of the presence of emotions. St. Basil even contended that a good Christian should not even laugh, because laughter is a form of emotion. Thus the new system of notation for music contained no symbols to represent the emotions and so today, 1,000 years later, we have not a single symbol whatsoever for feelings or emotion, even though that is the very purpose of music!

Because of this transformation of what is meant by "music" by the Church, the result was to use modern language to make music rational, part of the left hemisphere of the brain. The notation of music is a misnomer, for strictly speaking it is only the notation of the grammar of music. There is no real music on the page, as Mahler was careful to point out, "The important part of music is not found in the notes."

As a result, in music education we are teaching only half of what music is. We all make a distinction between hearing someone who "just plays the notes" and someone who we say is "musical." But we do not teach this distinction. It makes aesthetic adjudication in music impossible. Look at the adjudication sheet and you will see mostly the left hemisphere data words: intonation, balance, dynamics, etc., but where is the adjudication form which asks "Was this performance musical?" That question, the most important thing which can be adjudicated, is missing because of how we teach. The implication is that if all those left brain data points are correct then the performance will be musical. But that is not true, is it?

The music educator's very nomenclature becomes an illusion. We say we are teaching rhythm, but we are teaching arithmetic and it is no wonder the student has difficulty *feeling* rhythm when it is taught for the eye. We say we are teaching music when we teach harmony, but we are actually teaching how to read and understand a graphic foreign language. Harmony is not music, it is grammar. Indeed, the concept of teaching for the eye intrudes upon our very language, as we say, "Now, watch the intonation at letter B," while it is *hearing* the intonation at letter B which matters.

Just teaching *about* Music has never worked.

> Nothing is more futile than theorizing about music.
>   —Heinrich Heine, 1837

> Nothing is more difficult than to speak about music.
>   —Saint-Saëns, 1903

> The notion that you can educate a child musically by any other means whatsoever except than of having beautiful music finely performed within its hearing, is a notion which I feel constrained to denounce.
>   —George Bernard Shaw, *Music in London,* 1890–1894

Whatever part of American music education still honored teaching through performance, a dramatic event occurred on 4 October 1957, an event which changed the world: the launching of Sputnik I, the first man-made satellite, by the Soviet Union. The immediate result in America was a demand for more money for science and mathematics. I remember my music education teachers at Michigan at that moment became immediately fearful that this sudden change in national priorities would result in the loss of national support for music education.

In 1959 the American Council of Learned Societies and the American Musicological Society formed committees to improve music education. Nothing much was accomplished by either effort. At this time the National Science Foundation (NSF) set up a meeting in New York City to see if something could be done to help music education in the public schools. The NSF had no funds to support such a study, so the US Office of Education came forward with a large grant to sponsor a

Yale Seminar on Music Education in 1963. The purpose of the Yale Seminar was to analyze school music and to propose improvements. The Seminar, held for twelve days in June and July 1963, had its emphasis on musicality, stimulating creativity, composition and performance. Performance activities should be balanced among all groups and repertoire should be more contemporary, including jazz and non-Western music. The most interesting thing about this seminar of concerned intellectuals, composers, musicologists and critics was that no music educators were invited to participate! This Yale Seminar did not produce any tangible results, but it did gain publicity and put the emphasis on *music itself*, rather than being occupied with teaching methods as an end result.

The fact that no music education specialists had been invited to the Yale Seminar, resulted, as much from anger as anything else, in their organizing a new gathering called the Tanglewood Symposium of 1967. After much talking and discussion these distinguished music educators agreed on the following:

1. Music serves best when its integrity as an art is maintained.

2. Music of all periods, styles, forms and cultures belongs in the curriculum. The musical repertory should be expanded to involve music of our time in its rich variety, including currently popular teenage music and avant-garde music, American folk music and the music of other cultures.

3. Schools and colleges should provide adequate time for music in programs ranging from preschool through adult or continuing education.

4. Instruction in the arts should be a general and important part of education in the senior high school.

5. Developments in educational technology, educational television, programmed instruction, and computer-assisted instruction should be applied to music study and research.

6. Greater emphasis should be placed on helping the individual student to fulfill his needs, goals and potentials.

7. The music education profession must contribute its skills, proficiencies, and insights toward assisting in the solution of urgent social problems as in the "inner city" or other areas with culturally deprived individuals.

8. Programs of teacher education must be expanded and improved to provide music teachers who are specially equipped to teach high school courses in the history and literature of music, courses in the humanities and related arts, as well as teachers equipped to work with the very young, with adults, with disadvantaged, and with emotionally disturbed.

Well you don't see the word "performance" there so I, at least, have to wonder where "Music" fit into their thinking. There is not space here to detail the many conferences which followed, all seeking a more conceptual form of music teaching.

But there is another point of view. In an era where school children want music, to hear music, to make music and to perform music, MENC has discouraged this and attempted to replace it with left hemisphere literary concepts which are of very little interest to school children. And so today the children go home and teach themselves to play instruments, to sing and to compose. Finally, one cannot honestly evaluate the results of the shift to conceptual music teaching which began with the 1967 Tanglewood Symposium without considering the following facts:

• During the 1970s the participation of high school students in music courses declined from 25.1 to 21.6 percent, and fell even more during the 1980s. [*The American School Board Journal*, December, 1988, p. 15]

• A 1985 survey by the National Endowment for the Arts found:

  – 61% of adults do not attend one cultural event per year.

- 80% of adults have never had a music appreciation course, yet

- 25% [57 million!!] of adults played an instrument

• A 1991 Report of the National Commission on Music Education (Reston: MENC, 1991) found:

- In student-teacher ratio in music, South Dakota ranked best at 151:1 and California last at 1,535:1

- Only 15% of California music classes were taught by a qualified music teacher.

The challenge for the generation of the readers of this book is to find a way to make performance once again the central focus of music education, for as Wagner pointed out,

> The invisible bond, uniting the various branches of study, will always have to be performance.[182]

[182] "A Music School for Munich," in *Richard Wagner's Prose Works*, (New York: Broude, 1966), IV, 197.

My personal philosophy is that music education in the schools should be focused on the right hemisphere of the student's brain, on helping the student come to understand himself and learn to express himself with respect to the experiential and emotional side of himself. This is something no other school subject can accomplish as well, if at all. This would be such a contribution to humanity that it would at long last make music a core subject in the curriculum. Great minds have given testimony to this.

> Music ... lets us gaze into the inmost Essence of ourselves.
> —Richard Wagner[183]

[183] Wagner, Ellis, *Wagner's Prose Works*, V, 72.

> Music is to me the perfect expression of the soul.
> —Robert Schumann[184]

[184] Schumann, letter to his mother, Leipzig, May 8, 1832.

Music education based on performance would also open up additional areas of personal growth not possible under today's version of conceptual education, such as spirituality, character and manners.[185]

Time will not permit me to be the one who promotes this basic change in how we teach music, but the importance of returning performance to the central role of music education seems to me evident in this syllogism:

The central meaning and purpose of Music is found in the right hemisphere of the brain.

The right hemisphere is the half of the brain where the real child as an *individual* is found.

If the purpose of music is to educate the *individual* child, then music education must be centered in the right hemisphere of the child's brain.

What could be more clear?

[185] I have written a book on these and the entire issue of performance based music education. [Whitwell, *American Music Education: the Enigma and the Solution*, Whitwell Books, 2016]

About the Author

DR. DAVID WHITWELL is a graduate ("with distinction") of the University of Michigan and the Catholic University of America, Washington, D.C. (PhD, Musicology, Distinguished Alumni Award, 2000) and has studied conducting with Eugene Ormandy and at the Akademie für Musik, Vienna. Prior to coming to Northridge, Dr. Whitwell participated in concerts throughout the United States and Asia as Associate First Horn in the USAF Band and Orchestra in Washington DC, and in recitals throughout South America in cooperation with the United States State Department.

At the California State University, Northridge, which is in Los Angeles, Dr. Whitwell developed the CSUN Wind Ensemble into an ensemble of international reputation, with international tours to Europe in 1981 and 1989 and to Japan in 1984. The CSUN Wind Ensemble has made professional studio recordings for BBC (London), the Köln Westdeutscher Rundfunk (Germany), NOS National Radio (The Netherlands), Zürich Radio (Switzerland), the Television Broadcasting System (Japan) as well as for the United States State Department for broadcast on its "Voice of America" program. The CSUN Wind Ensemble's recording with the Mirecourt Trio in 1982 was named the "Record of the Year" by *The Village Voice*. Composers who have guest conducted Whitwell's ensembles include Aaron Copland, Ernest Krenek, Alan Hovhaness, Morton Gould, Karel Husa, Frank Erickson and Vaclav Nelhybel.

Dr. Whitwell has been a guest professor in 100 different universities and conservatories throughout the United States and in twenty-three foreign countries (most recently in China, in an elite school housed in the Forbidden City). Guest conducting experiences have included the Philadelphia Orchestra, Seattle Symphony Orchestra, the Czech Radio Orchestras of Brno and Bratislava, The National Youth Orchestra of Israel, as well as resident wind ensembles in Russia, Israel, Austria, Switzerland, Germany, England, Wales, The Netherlands, Portugal, Peru, Korea, Japan, Taiwan, Canada and the United States.

He is a past president of the College Band Directors National Association, a member of the Prasidium of the International Society for the Promotion of Band Music, and was a member of the founding board of directors of the World Association for Symphonic Bands and Ensembles (WASBE). In 1964 he was made an honorary life member of Kappa Kappa Psi, a national professional music fraternity. In September, 2001, he was a delegate to the UNESCO Conference on Global Music in Tokyo. He has been knighted by sovereign organizations in France, Portugal and Scotland and has been awarded the gold medal of Kerkrade, The Netherlands, and the silver medal of Wangen, Germany, the highest honor given wind conductors in the United States, the medal of the Academy of Wind and Percussion Arts (National Band Association) and the highest honor given wind conductors in Austria, the gold medal of the Austrian Band Association. He is a member of the Hall of Fame of the California Music Educators Association.

Dr. Whitwell's publications include more than 127 articles on wind literature including publications in *Music and Letters* (London), the *London Musical Times,* the *Mozart-Jahrbuch* (Salzburg), and 50 books, among which is his 13-volume *History and Literature of the Wind Band and Wind Ensemble* and an 8-volume series on *Aesthetics in Music.* In addition to numerous modern editions of early wind band music his original compositions include five symphonies.

David Whitwell was named as one of six men who have
determined the course of American bands during the second
half of the twentieth century, in the definitive history, *The
Twentieth Century American Wind Band* (Meredith Music). A
doctoral dissertation by German Gonzales (2007, Arizona State
University) is dedicated to the life and conducting career of
David Whitwell through the year 1977. David Whitwell is one
of nine men described by Paula A. Crider in *The Conductor's
Legacy* (Chicago: GIA, 2010) as "the legendary conductors" of
the twentieth century.

> "I can't imagine the 2nd half of the 20th century—without
> David Whitwell and what he has given to all of the rest of us."
> Frederick Fennell (1993)